A Perfect Union

of Patchwork & Appliqué

DARLENE C. CHRISTOPHERSON

C&T PUBLISHING INC.

© 2003 Darlene Christopherson
Editor-in-Chief: Darra Williamson
Editor: Kerry Smith
Technical Editors: Peggy Kass, Joyce Engels Lytle
Proofreader: Carol Barrett
Cover Designer: Aliza Kahn Shalit
Book Designer: Staci Harpole, Cubic Design
Design Director: Diane Pedersen
Illustrator: Richard Sheppard
Production Assistants: Jeff Carrillo, Luke Mulks
Quilt Photography: Bob Smith/Accurate Image of Waco, Texas
How-to Photography: C&T Publishing, Inc.
Published by C&T Publishing, Inc., P.O. Box 1456, Lafayette, California 94549

Front cover: *A Perfect Union* by Darlene C. Christopherson
Back cover: *Blue Birds of Paradise* by Nellie Bomer, *Stars and Its Many Wonders* by Fran Snay and Nancy KcKannon

Attention Copy Shops: Please note the following exception—Publisher and author give permission to photocopy pages 12—14, 35—50, 67—72, 78, 84—85, 92—93, and 99 for personal use only.

Attention Teachers: C&T Publishing, Inc. encourages you to use this book as a text for teaching. Contact us at 800-284-1114 or www.ctpub.com for more information about the C&T Teachers Program.

We take great care to ensure that the information included in this book is accurate and presented in good faith, but no warranty is provided nor results guaranteed. Since we have no control over the choices of materials or procedures used, neither the author nor C&T Publishing, Inc. shall have any liability to any person or entity with respect to any loss or damage caused directly or indirectly by the information contained in this book. For your convenience, we post an up-to-date listing of corrections on our web page (www.ctpub.com). If a correction is not already noted, please contact our customer service department at ctinfo@ctpub.com or at P.O. Box 1456, Lafayette, CA 94549.

Trademarked (™) and Registered Trademark (®) names are used throughout this book. Rather than use the symbols with every occurrence of a trademark and registered trademark name, we are using the names only in the editorial fashion and to the benefit of the owner, with no intention of infringement.

Library of Congress Cataloging-in-Publication Data

Christopherson, Darlene C. (Darlene Celeste)
  A perfect union of patchwork and appliqué / Darlene C. Christopherson.
     p. cm.
Includes index.
  ISBN 1-57120-197-1 (paper trade)
  1. Appliqué--Patterns. 2. Patchwork--Patterns. 3. Quilts. I. Title.
  TT779 .C486 2003
  746.46'041--dc21
                          2002013370

Printed in China
10 9 8 7 6 5 4 3 2 1

CONTENTS

Dedication 4

Acknowledgments 4

Foreword 5

Introduction 6

Chapter One: **Planning Your Quilt** 8

Chapter Two: **Fabric Selection** 18

Chapter Three: **Appliqué** 26

Chapter Four: **Patchwork** 54

Chapter Five: **Evening Star** 60

Chapter Six: **Eight-Pointed Star** 74

Chapter Seven: **Mariner's Compass** 81

Chapter Eight: **Sashing** 88

Chapter Nine: **Borders** 94

Chapter Ten: **Hand Quilting** 101

Chapter Eleven: **Finishing** 107

Resources 110

About the Author 111

Index 111

In loving memory of Alfred G. Christopherson married to Helen for 55 years.

In honor and respect for Irwin J. and Charlotte B. Aasen, my parents. All my life my dad told me to tell everyone who my daddy is.

In hopes for another perfect union for my daughter Pilar and her husband Todd Gibson.

In gratitude for my husband Douglas.

Empty Nest
**Hand pieced and quilted by
Darlene Christopherson the
year Pilar left home**
29" x 29"

D E D I C A T I O N   &   A C K N O W L E D G M E N T S

ACKNOWLEDGMENTS

Thank you to the following ladies who gathered with me to share the quilting lessons that I have learned. I value your participation, always.

Gayle King, Deborah Fugitt, Dorothy Vanderbilt, Kathy Barker, Osie Lebowitz, Jo Griffitt, Shirley Pinkston, Teresa Tolbert, Patty Pinkston, Vicki Kelley, Joan Northern, Cheryl Kyle, Maxie Jones, Lynah Egenberger, Fran Snay, Alice Richardson, Janie McClain, Colleen Barnes, Inga-Lill Westblom, Larrain Greer, Patsy Autmon, Nite Benoit, Nellie Bomer, Dorothy Conder, Leola Eaton, Karen Eacrett, Nancy Farmer, Terri Gant, Tommie Gilbreath, Rosie Gohl, Sandy Kearney, Cathy Letson, Bernice Lindley, Sharon Moses, Mary Pinson, Anita Smith, Athalie Southard, Judy Michalk, Karen Bacon, Trixie Bitterie-Ortiz, Maryette Clifton, Laura Herbst, Diana Howell, Terri Masquelier, Rhe Northcutt, Shirley Porter, Angie Purvis, Eleanor Rainwater, Nancy Schoenemann, Shirley Thomas, Lynda Sue Wooten, Dawn Smith, Mattie Ehler, Patsy Biggs, Alice Watkins, Pat Schuler, Gladys Keith, Ophelia Christian, Janet Flink, Bonnie Cadwell, June Randall, Alice Person, Carol Cayard, Jan Taylor, Margaret Sowden, Susan Nelson, Jo Ivie, Kathy Jones, Eloise Chuber, Becky Hernandez, Pam Frazier, Louise Eller, Sandi McMahill, June Holt, Joyce Orr, Yvonne Jordon, LaTrelle Power, Cathy Ekholm, Karen Roxburgh, Jan Wilson, Janell Scott, Martha Crump, Linda Dyer, Debbie Mahaney, Diane Kamego, Jackie Gilmer, Nancy Brown, Joan Jones, Carol Bramlett, Betty Bell, Sally Coble, Judy Chapman, Phyllis Osborn, Joy Fontenot, Sue Cary, Flo Bayne, Lou DeMott, Patti Vesenious, Pat Riddile, Carol Ann Beimer, Lee Rash, Yvonne Ables, Tracer Moyer, Terri Allen, Donna Bardwell, Kay May, Mildred Carr, Yoko Cotton, Alicia Vander Fliet, Sonnie Goar, Jane Giller, and Jo Pittman

FOREWORD

My love for the combination of patchwork and appliqué started early in my quiltmaking life. While I was living in the Washington, DC area, I visited the Daughters of the American Revolution (DAR) Museum where quilts are shared year round. Collections from the Smithsonian Museum, Baltimore Historical Society, and local shows, all of which included quilts from the 1800s, allowed me to observe the elements of design, including color, value, balance, line, pattern, contrast, accent, and texture.

My first instructor was Anna Dean Holland in historic Leesburg, Virginia. Anna taught me hand piecing, quilting, and introduced me to appliqué. She instilled in me a love for red and green, the mellow nature of the color brown, and the glorious combination of stars and appliqué in quilts. My quilt, *Anna's Influence*, is named for her. We are good friends to this day.

Anna's Influence

Hand pieced and quilted by
Darlene Christopherson
50" x 50"

Jinny Beyer was a neighbor, and her first book and line of fabrics inspired my commitment to a lifetime of quiltmaking. In 1989, after taking her classes, I joined the staff of her Hilton Head Island Seminar. I treasured the meetings where staff members shared ideas and encouraged each other.

Noted appliqué instructor Elly Sienkiewicz taught near my home and I attended her classes. These and many other fine teachers left an indelible mark on my quiltmaker's mind.

I've since made many quilts combining the graphic qualities of patchwork and the pictorial essence of appliqué. More recently, I introduced a series of eight classes named "A Perfect Union: The Combination of Patchwork and Appliqué." The classes were popular, when the phrases "bird parts" and "striking addition" were overheard in local quilt shops students recognized each other, and shared their experiences.

Many students made their first quilts in these classes. Dawn Smith made her last. My blue and brown quilt *Dawn's Influence* (page 73), was named in her honor. Maxie Jones finished her quilt so quickly it was as though she knew her time was short. Others used the series to carry them through cancer treatments and other life challenges.

Joan Northern developed her quilt around the theme of Queen Victoria and Prince Albert. Joan's quilt label includes the words that the queen spoke at her husband's funeral: "Ours was a perfect union, both in love and admiration, as well as unification of our countries." Colleen Barnes made a quilt as a special wedding gift for her granddaughter. Fran Snay, an avid machine piecer, was converted to hand appliqué.

We held a number of "Perfect Re-Unions" to share our quilts and applaud the different results we achieved with the same basic designs. We shared pride and encouragement as our quilts grew. I hope that this book encourages you to join or create a group to follow the lessons, enjoy the friendships, and flourish. You may even form a group on the Internet. Set deadlines and share pictures via your computer screens. How far we have come from the days of exchanging brown paper templates from the back of a covered wagon!

Darlene C. Christopherson

INTRODUCTION

*Invite friends
to join you
on your
quiltmaking
journey.*

One of the most rewarding things about my quiltmaking journey is that it includes gathering with friends in a class setting or bee. I've gained a great deal from these collective experiences and offer the lessons and patterns in this book in the hope that you will learn the techniques together with friends. The appliqué and patchwork blocks and sashing and border designs are interchangeable so no two quilts will be the same.

Quilts appear throughout the book to inspire you. Take the time to browse before making any decisions. Read Chapter Two (page 18) to learn about the basic elements of design. Mix one, two, or three types of patchwork blocks with your favorite appliqué blocks. If you prefer, make an all-appliqué or all-patchwork quilt—the choice is yours. The sashing options, combined with one of three borders will balance and enhance your sampling of blocks.

In Chapters Ten (page 101) and Eleven (page 107) I've included a few basics to help you quilt and finish your quilt. Resources (page 110) lists instructors, manufacturers, and a few shops where you can find the tools, products, and information that I mention.

Invite friends—either local or online—to join you on your quiltmaking journey. Set deadlines and challenges, schedule retreats, and form quilt book clubs. Explore lessons and patterns. In the end, you each will have a great quilt and a marvelous experience.

I would love to hear from you! Tell me how your "Perfect Union" project develops and share photos of your quilts via my website, www.darlenechristopherson.com. There you will also find links to some of my favorite quilting-related websites, and information about my lectures and workshops.

A Perfect Union

Hand pieced and hand quilted by Darlene Christopherson

66 $\frac{1}{2}$" x 66 $\frac{1}{2}$"

PLANNING YOUR QUILT

*Create a
balanced quilt
that combines
patchwork and
appliqué!*

I n this chapter, I provide basic information about planning and yardage for your quilt. Use the information as a starting point then start planning your own unique and interesting combination of patchwork and appliqué!

Layouts

A block-set quilt needs balance. In the planning stage, determine what type of blocks you want to include in your quilt. If you prefer to appliqué as many blocks as possible, but want to include some pieced blocks for added interest, then choose the appliqué blocks first. Place a special block in the center. Balance the visual weight by placing an Eight-Pointed Star in each of the four corners, or cutwork blocks in the center of each of the four sides of the quilt. Keep in mind that even an off-centered design needs some degree of balance. Study *Blue Birds of Paradise* (page 100) for an example of an off-center design, and *The Perfect Union—My Salvation* (page 17) for an example of a centered design.

Finished Quilt Sizes

Sashing Option One

	Center	With Borders
9 blocks	34" x 34"	50" x 50"
12 blocks	34" x 44"	50" x 60"
25 Blocks	54" x 54"	70" x 70"

Sashing Options Two through Five

	Center	With Borders
9 blocks	32" x 32"	48" x 48"
12 blocks	32" x 42"	48" x 58"
25 blocks	52" x 52"	68" x 68"

Cut and Paste a Quilt Plan

Photocopy the layout of your choice (pages 12–14). Cut the desired number of blocks and use a glue stick to fasten them to the layout diagram. Use this mock-up as a tool to place fabrics and plan your quilt. Later, as you sew the sections, you can rearrange the blocks or make others that you like better.

Yardage

All blocks in this book finish 8" square. All sashing finishes 2" x 8", and cornerstones finish 2" square. All borders finish 8" wide. Sashing Option One adds a 1" pieced sash of background fabric in order to extend the stars into the border.

If you think you want to use the same fabric for the block and border backgrounds, purchase all the fabric before you begin making blocks. Set aside the amount needed for the borders. Purchase fabrics for the appliqué, pieced blocks, sashing, and border appliqué in small quantities until you have made a few blocks, and are happy with the direction of your design. Additional fabrics can be added as the quilt grows.

If you decide to make Evening Star blocks, and wish to repeat certain fabrics (e.g. star points) in every block, then purchase the entire amount required at one time. See *Dawn's Influence* (page 73).

Yardage is based on 40"-wide, 100% cotton fabric. As some fabrics are repeated in blocks, sashing, and borders, total them carefully before you go to your quilt shop or stash! Yardages given yield binding strips with minimal joining seams. If you don't mind piecing strips for binding, you will need less fabric.

	9-Block	12-Block	25-Block
Block background	1 yard	1 yard	2 yards
Border background	1 5/8 yard	1 7/8 yards	2 yards
Blocks (all)	12⁺ fat quarters	16⁺ fat quarters	18⁺ fat quarters
Evening Star (points)	1/2 yard	5/8 yard	1 yard
Sashing options			
Template A	1/4 yard	1/4 yard	3/8 yard
Template B	1/3 yard	3/8 yard	5/8 yard
Templates C or D	1/2 yard	3/4 yard	1 1/4 yard
Templates E (2 colors)	1/2 yard each	1 yard each	1 1/8 yards each
Templates F (2 colors)	1/2 yard each	5/8 yard each	7/8 yard each
Template G (background)	1/4 yard	1/3 yard	1/3 yard
Template H (background)	1 fat quarter	1/8 yard	1/8 yard
Template I & N (background)	1/8 yard	1/8 yard	1/8 yard
Border options			
Swag*	1 1/3 yards	1 1/3 yards	1 1/2 yards
Teardrop	1 fat quarter	1 fat quarter	1 fat quarter
Dogtooth**	1 5/8 yards	1 7/8 yards	2 1/8 yards
Vine	1 yard	1 yard	1 yard
Leaves	scraps from blocks	scraps from blocks	scraps from blocks
Backing (40" wide)	3 1/3 yards	4 yards	4 1/2 yards
Backing (108" wide)	1 2/3 yards	2 yards	2 1/4 yards
Bias Binding	3/4 yard	3/4 yard	3/4 yard
Straight Binding	1/2 yard	5/8 yard	5/8 yard

* Yardage is for evenly placed swags and will vary depending on the direction of the print and frequency of repeat. Add extra yardage for repeats as needed. See page 22.
** Includes enough yardage for straight-grain binding.

Tools and Supplies

See Resources on page 110 for additional information.

Needles and Pins

I recommend the following needles and pins:

Appliqué needles, Richard Hemming & Son Milliners #11

Basting needles, John James Darners #9

Quilting needles, EZ Gold Eye Betweens #12

Hand-piecing needles, Gold Eye Appliqué Sharps #11

Fine, headless silk pins such as those made by Clover or IBC

Flower-head pins

Thread

I recommend the following threads:

YLI basting thread for basting

YLI quilting threads for quilting

Mettler 60/2 cotton thread for hand appliqué

Mettler 50/3 cotton thread for hand and machine piecing

Marking Pencils and Pens

You'll need a mechanical pencil, and a silver and/or white art pencil. (My favorite brand is Verithin.) You'll also need a fine-tip or ultra-fine tip permanent marker.

Scissors

You'll need three pairs of scissors: one for fabric, one small pair for appliqué (I recommend Gingher 4" embroidery scissors), and one for cutting paper and template materials.

Lightbox

A lightbox makes it very easy to transfer appliqué patterns to template materials and fabrics. Instructions to follow.

Template Materials

Template plastic and freezer paper are essential. Pre-made templates are also available.

Rotary Cutting Tools

You will need a rotary cutter, acrylic rulers (12 1/2" square and 6" x 24"), and a cutting mat.

Hand-Quilting Supplies

Refer to Hand Quilting (page 104) for supplies and tools.

Miscellaneous

Glue stick

A few file folders

Metal pencil sharpener

Wallpaper knife (with a break away, retractable blade)

Scotch brand removable tape

Scotch brand magic tape (1/2" or 3/4" wide)

Masking tape (3/4" or 1" wide)

Clover brand HERA marking tool (marks fabrics with a crease)

Clover Tape Maker

Clover seam ripper with long handle

Sandpaper marking board (purchase one, or make one with a sheet of fine sandpaper, adhered to a file folder or board)

1/16" Hole punch

Iron

Teflon appliqué pressing sheet (optional, but helpful for pressing fusible batting)

Large pressing surface (see below)

Make a Lightbox

To make a lightbox, invert a 5" deep, flat-bottomed 15" x 22" clear plastic sweater storage box over a fluorescent tube or a cool light, such as an Ott-Lite bulb. Do not use a halogen lamp. When attending a class, pack your supplies in the box for transport.

Make a Large Pressing Surface

Purchase a pre-cut 30" x 48" piece of plywood, or a size that fits your workspace, at a hardware store or lumberyard. They will cut the board for you if necessary. In addition, you'll need two 30" x 48" pieces of 100% cotton or 80/20% blend fusible batting, household aluminum foil, one yard of 54"-wide ticking, and a staple gun. (Ticking is wider than most cotton fabrics, and is especially durable. Colorfast decorator fabric is another good choice.)

1. Lay the ticking right side down on a flat surface.

2. Add and center the 2 layers of batting over the ticking. Smooth each layer as you go.

3. Add a layer of foil, then the plywood.

4. With the help of a friend, pull the ticking tightly over the plywood at opposite ends, fold the fabric twice and staple. Repeat on the other two sides.

Cut and Paste a Quilt Plan

Photocopy the quilt layouts and blocks. Follow the
instructions on page 9.

instructions on page 9.

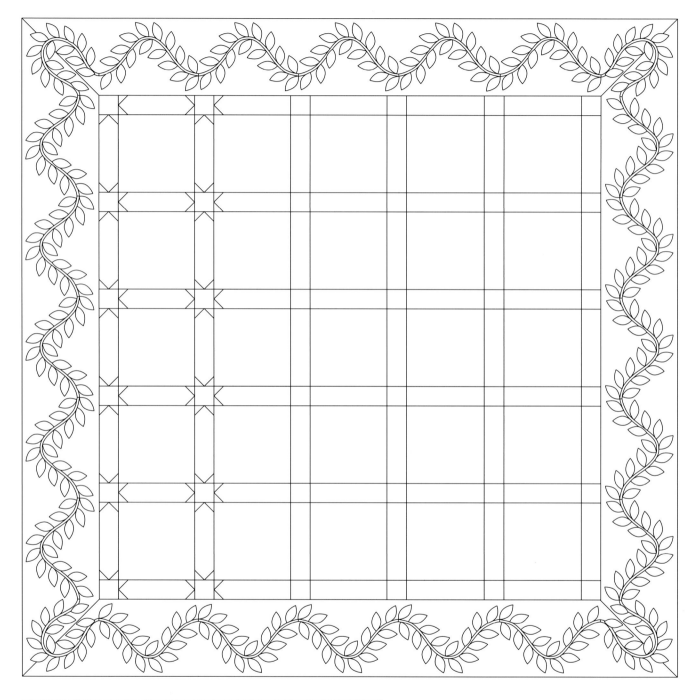

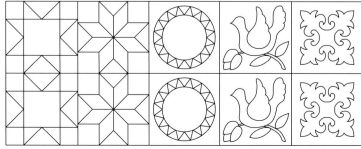

25-Block quilt layout with
Leaf and Vine border option

PLANNING YOUR QUILT

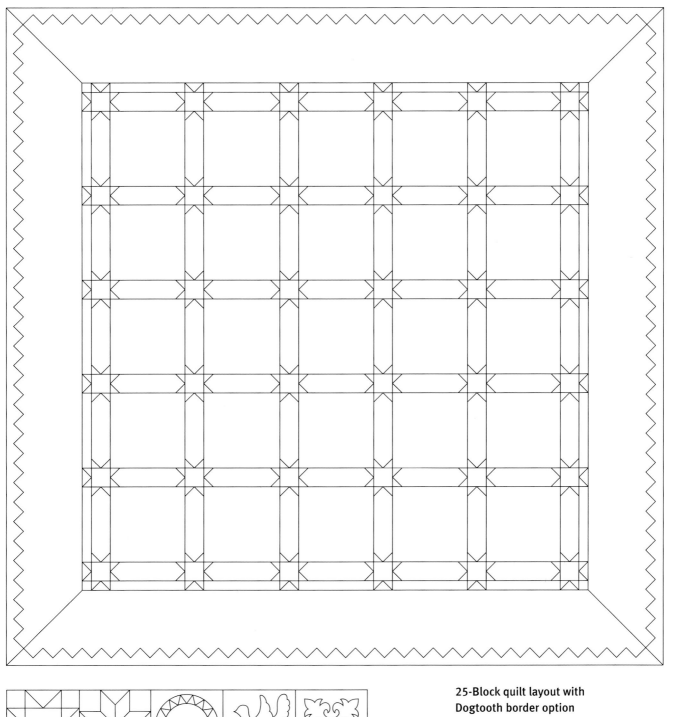

25-Block quilt layout with
Dogtooth border option

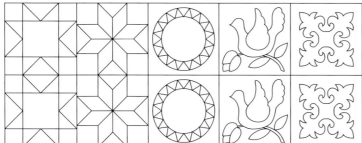

25-Block quilt layout with Swag
and Teardrop border option

Perfectly Challenging

Pieced and hand quilted
by Alice Person

47" x 47"

**Stars and Its
Many Wonders**

Pieced by Fran Snay,
machine quilted
by Nancy McKannon

53" x 53"

**A Perfect Union—
Jennifer and Taylor**

Pieced by Colleen Barnes,
machine quilted by Molly Culp

84" x 84"

**The Perfect Union—
My Salvation**

Pieced by Bonnie Oltmann, machine
quilted by Keith Oltmann

72" x 72"

FABRIC SELECTION

Fabrics play a major role in the success of a quilt's design.

If the quiltmakers who preceded us had made only red, white, and blue schoolhouse quilts, the art of quiltmaking would have died out long ago. Instead, the diversity in their quilts inspires us with a range of lessons for successful quiltmaking.

There is no formula for assigning importance to any single design element, but fabric selection plays a major role in the success of any design. Fabric choice also expresses the individuality of the quiltmaker. This book offers a unique approach to creating quilts that express your individuality, with my work—and that of my students—as inspiration. The rest is up to you!

When selecting fabric, it is important to create visual contrast. For example, you can create visual contrast from one patchwork piece to another, from one block to another, or between an appliqué design and its background, or within parts of a flower or bird motif. The degree of importance placed on each element of the design is a strictly personal choice.

Decide on a theme, or "look," for your quilt, and then add to the fabric assortment as the quilt grows—the more choices the merrier! In most cases, increasing the number of fabrics in a quilt reduces the importance of each individual fabric. The greater the number of blocks, the greater the number of fabrics you can use. See *Midnight Madness* quilt (page 52).

The Basics

Visual differences create interest. The areas in which to consider contrast in fabrics are value, color, and texture.

Value

Value, that is the relative lightness or darkness of the fabric, is used to accentuate the graphic design found in patchwork. It enables pictorial and cutwork appliqué images to stand out from the backgrounds to which they are applied, and enhances appliqué motifs by adding depth and interest. Note the fabrics that are arranged from light to dark in the following discussion about color.

Color

Color is the most personal choice you'll make when selecting fabric. Always begin with colors that appeal to you.

Color offers a contrast when you are using fabric close in value, intensity, or brightness. You can also use the contrast between cool (green, blue, purple) and warm colors (red, orange, yellow) to separate pieces in patchwork or appliqué.

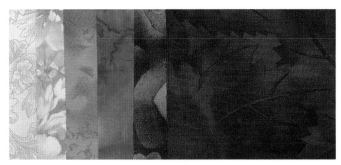

Two cool colors, from light to dark

One warm color, from light to dark

Texture

Have you ever wanted to touch a quilt knowing that you really shouldn't? This is a natural sensory reaction to visual texture. An architect or interior decorator may use a well-balanced selection of metals, textiles, wood, glass, and tile to achieve textural differences. As quiltmakers, we can express textural differences with the fabrics that we select. Fabric print characteristics can provide a wide range of textures, depending on the lines, shape, or scale of the printed motif.

Geometric Pattern

Geometric pattern is a uniformly repeated visual characteristic which you can manipulate to create movement over the surface of your quilt.

Motif is repeated creating a geometric appearance.

Directional and border prints are literally striped, or give the illusion of stripes or direction. You can add visual interest to simple patchwork patterns by including directional and border prints, to accentuate a radiating design or outline a particular print. Jinny Beyer's directional prints have been a staple of mine since my early years of quiltmaking. You can cut an excellent appliquéd vase from a border print! See *A Few of My Favorite Things* (page 53).

Assorted directional and border prints

Large-Scale Prints

I like to use large-scale prints for cutwork, or in the center
of an Evening Star or Sunflower block where the space is
large enough to showcase the enlarged motif. These prints
work well for appliqués, too. I am always searching for
prints to use as bird parts, baskets, vases, trees, leaves, and
flower petals. A well-chosen fabric can suggest maximum
detail with little effort. A bird part needn't always be cut
from "feather" fabric; often a paisley or floral print
includes a special element that contributes to a unique
species of appliqué bird, known to my students as
"ornamentus picturesque-tus." Look carefully at fabrics to
find "hidden treasures" that can be used to create specific
pictorial effects.

Fabrics for leaves

Fabrics for bird parts

Using fabrics for leaves

**Using fabrics for
bird wings, tails,
and bodies**

Large-scale print fabrics

Do you see a bird's nest in the bear?

Accents

An accent is an element such as color, value, or texture that adds visual interest. It generally offers some contrast to the rest of the fabrics you select, and should be used sparingly, what begins as an accent can quickly become overwhelming. Compare your fabric selection to a bread recipe, which includes many ingredients in varying amounts. The bread would not taste the same if each ingredient were measured in equal amounts. Also, if one of the ingredients, such as the yeast, was left out, the bread would literally be flat. Consider accent fabrics in this manner. Their inclusion and their proportion are both important.

When a fabric is darker, stronger, bolder, lighter, brighter, or busier relative to other fabrics in the same grouping, I call it an "ER" or an accent fabric.

Relativity

The same fabric can function as a dark in one situation and a medium-light in another. The fabrics immediately surrounding the fabric in question determine its effect. In relationship to an adjacent light fabric, another light fabric could be considered dark.

The quilts in this book contain blocks separated by sashing, with additional borders. In this style quilt, all other fabrics are placed on, or next to, the background fabric. Therefore, the background fabric needs to be relatively lighter or darker in order to visually separate or contrast with them.

Depth

A rich, dark fabric enhances the illusion of depth in pictorial appliqué or pieced blocks. Remember: The darkness of a fabric is relative to the value of the other fabrics around it. It is not always necessary to use the absolute darkest value to attain depth. For example, see the dark green fabric on page 19.

"Known Factor" Fabrics

Generally, when I start planning a new quilt project, I begin with one favorite fabric. I call that fabric my "known factor." This fabric may include two or three colors, and becomes the basis for my other fabric selections.

A known factor (or focus fabric) is an excellent point at which to start collecting fabrics for your quilts. Add an assortment of other fabrics that will both enhance and contrast in value, color, and texture. The goal is to accentuate and compliment the known factor. Try not to repeat elements, such as color, that are present in your known factor fabric.

Background Fabrics

The background fabric provides a canvas or foundation for all the other fabrics you select for your quilt. If you decide to use the same fabric throughout, you should purchase the entire required yardage at one time. If you prefer a variety of fabrics, such as a range of neutrals, you can add fabrics as your quilt grows.

If your goal is to make a bold statement, choose a background fabric in high contrast to the other fabrics in your quilt. If you prefer a softer look, reduce the contrast between the background and other fabrics. (A mellow light to medium-light often creates a subtle effect.) Study *Perfectly Challenging* (page 15) and *Red Birds of Happiness* (page 87) to see the effect background fabrics have on the overall quilt.

Sashing and Cornerstone Fabrics

The scale and texture of sashing and cornerstone fabrics should coordinate, not compete, with the appliqué and patchwork blocks. Choose fabrics that enhance and unify the blocks, as well as frame them.

Chapter Eight (page 88) includes five options for sashing your blocks. Once you have created several blocks, place them on the fabrics that you are considering for sashing and cornerstones. This is the perfect opportunity to incorporate accent or "ER" fabrics. Cornerstones are especially fine locations for "ER" fabrics; they are small and repeat at every block intersection. For inspiration, see *Never Say Never* (page 58).

Border Fabrics

You can select your border fabric at any time while making the blocks. However, if you want to use a favorite fabric in the quilt blocks and border, you must make your choice early and purchase the entire yardage at that time. Be sure to choose a fabric (or fabrics) that frame the body of the quilt nicely, and repeat, accentuate, or enhance some element of the overall design.

Swag Border

The Swag border allows you to feature a large area of a favorite fabric. As such, this choice is a major decision. The small teardrops offer an excellent opportunity to use an "ER" fabric. You might even use the same fabric for the teardrops and cornerstones. This unifies the body of the quilt, extending an accent fabric out into the border. See *The Perfect Union* as an example (page 79).

Dogtooth Border

The Dogtooth border allows a generous area to showcase special quilting whether your own or those drawn from books or stencils. Choose a tightly woven fabric for the dogtooth motif as the design includes many inside and outside points. See *Dawn's Influence* (page 73).

Vine and Leaf Border

Repeat several favorite fabrics from the body of the quilt to make vines and leaves for the quilt border. This unifies the body of the quilt and the border—a useful device when your quilt includes many fabrics. See *Midnight Madness* (page 52) for inspiration.

KEYS TO SUCCESS!

If your fabric has acquired that "old closet" smell, punch a few holes in the lid of a plastic container and add baking soda or a few charcoal briquettes. Place the container in the area where the fabric is stored to filter the air and freshen the fabric. Change the baking soda or briquettes frequently.

Searching for Solace

Pieced and quilted by Jo Pittman

64" x 64"

**An Adventure into Appliqué
and Patchwork**

Pieced and quilted by Gladys Keith

67" x 67"

A Perfect Union Too

Pieced by Nancy Brown,
machine quilted by Linda Walsh

57" x 57"

3 APPLIQUÉ

*Appliqué
allows the
freedom
to stitch
any design
imaginable.*

The flowing curves of appliqué designs are a perfect compliment to the straight lines of patchwork. Appliqué offers freedom from seamline and precision issues, and all stitching is done with the design facing up. This chapter includes both cutwork and pictorial appliqué techniques and patterns. Once you have mastered the needle-turn stitch, there is no barrier to producing any design imaginable.

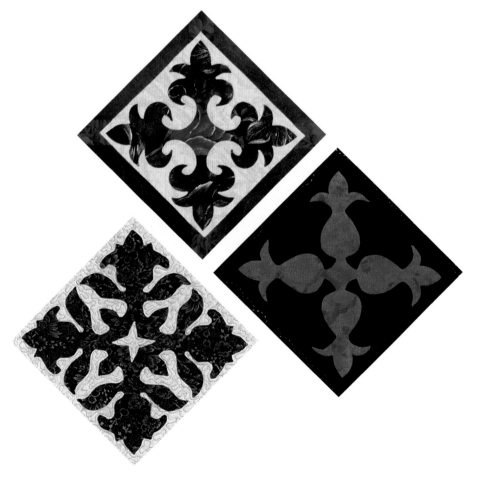

Cutwork Appliqué

A cutwork or "paper cut" appliqué is created by folding paper to make a pattern, which is then transferred to the appliqué fabric. This marked layer of fabric is layered over a background block, and then cut and stitched to expose the bottom or background layer.

Preparing Cutwork Blocks

The finished size of each block is 8" square. Press the fabric, then cut all background blocks 9" square on the straight grain of the fabric (parallel to the selvage edge). This will compensate for the fabric drawing up during appliqué. After completing the appliqué, you will trim the blocks to 8 1/2" square.

If you mark seamlines for the background blocks, then it is a good idea to mark seamlines for all other blocks, sashing, and borders in the quilt (see page 29). Note any directional print before you place and stitch your appliqué pieces to the blocks.

1. Using a rotary cutter, mat, and square ruler, cut one 9" square of background fabric and one 9" square of appliqué fabric for each cutwork block.

2. Use scissors or a rotary cutter to cut an 8" square of freezer paper. Fold the freezer paper in half with the coated sides together, and crease the folded edge. Repeat to fold the freezer paper into quarters, creating two folded and two cut edges. The uncoated side of the freezer paper will be on the outside.

3. Select a cutwork block and trace or photocopy the pattern (pages 35–36). Cut out the full, copied pattern square. Place the copied pattern on top of the folded freezer paper. Align the folded sides of the freezer paper with the word "fold" on the copied pattern. Staple the pattern and freezer paper together in several places within the design area to stabilize the layers.

4. Cut a freezer paper template, following the solid lines on the pattern. Remove the staples and unfold the freezer paper.

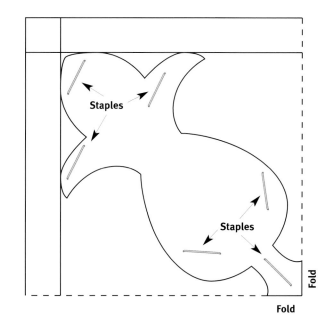

5. Fold the appliqué fabric square in half and then into quarters, lightly finger pressing each folded edge. Center the freezer paper template shiny side down on the right side of the appliqué fabric, aligning the folds in the template with the fabric creases. Press the template to the right side of the fabric square with a dry iron, on a medium setting.

6. Place the fabric square on a sandpaper board, and trace around the template with a silver or white marking pencil. Do not use a permanent marker. (In appliqué the drawn line on a pattern is the sewing line.)

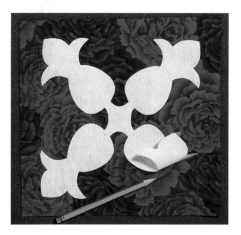

Trace around the template.

7. Remove the freezer paper template. Place the appliqué square right side up on the right side of the background square. Smooth, then pin the layers together, using four pins. Use contrasting color thread and $^1/_2$"-long stitches to baste the layers together. Stitches must be slightly more than $^1/_8$" inside the drawn seamline, so that you can turn the seam allowance easily when you appliqué. Remove the pins and make sure that the layered squares are smooth and flat.

Sew the appliqué to the background.

KEYS TO SUCCESS!

Use tightly woven fabric, which is easier to appliqué.
Good lighting is essential.
Use fresh, fine needles for even stitches.
Use short lengths of thread.
Keep a fresh cut on the thread end to reduce tangling.
Always stitch with clean hands.

Stitching

1. Starting on the straightest edge, cut through the top layer of appliqué fabric only, allowing a $^1/_8$"-wide seam allowance outside the drawn line. Do not cut more than 2" beyond the point where you will begin stitching.

Cut through the top layer only.

2. Sew the appliqué motif to the background square using the needle-turn stitch described on page 32. As you turn under the seam allowance, the background fabric is revealed.

3. Stitch until you are close to the point at which you stopped cutting, then cut another 2" ahead in the appliqué fabric. Continue stitching and cutting until you have appliquéd the entire motif, then press (page 34).

4. If you are using templates to mark seamlines for the patchwork blocks and sashing seams in your quilt, mark seamlines on the back of the block as described in Preparing Pictorial Background Blocks (page 29).

KEYS TO SUCCESS!

Uniformity makes all the difference! Add a consistent $^1/_8$" seam allowance when cutting the appliqué. Practice cutting neatly, echoing the penciled seamlines. Small, sharp embroidery scissors are essential.

Pictorial Appliqué

Pictorial appliqué features fabric shapes cut, positioned, and stitched to a background fabric to create a design that can vary from folk to representational art. Nature—such as birds and flowers—is a major source of inspiration, as are bowls of fruit, floral arrangements, or other stylized designs. If you can draw it, you can stitch it. I hope that you will see the world around you with a new perspective, and find joy in adapting what you see into beautiful appliqué blocks.

Preparing Pictorial Background Blocks

The finished size of each block is 8" square. Press the fabric then cut all background blocks 9" square on the straight grain of the fabric (parallel to the selvage edge) to compensate for the fabric drawing up during appliqué. After completing the appliqué, you will trim the blocks to 8½" square. Note any directional print before you place and stitch your appliqué pieces to the blocks.

Marked Seamline Method

If you mark seamlines for the background blocks, then it is a good idea to mark seamlines for all other blocks, sashing, and borders in the quilt.

1. Place the background fabric right side down on your cutting mat. Use a cutting ruler and mechanical pencil to draw two parallel lines 8" apart. Align the ruler with the first two marked lines to create and mark an 8" square. After completing the appliqué, cut out the block, adding a ¼"-wide seam allowance on all sides.

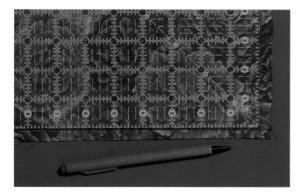

Mark the lines to create an 8" square.

Fold the fabric square in half, and then into quarters, aligning the marked seamlines and gently pressing the folds. These fold lines match the lines on the patterns and will be used for the placement of the appliqués.

Preparing Stems

Make all stems from bias strips. Use a rotary cutter, and cut all strips 1"-wide, unless otherwise noted. For best results, prepare all stems of one color in minimum 12" lengths and cut to size later.

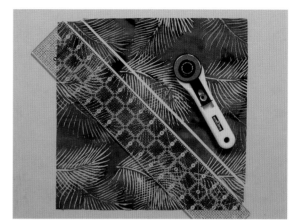

Cut 1"-wide bias strips.

1. Fold the bias strips in half lengthwise, wrong sides together, pressing with a dry iron to create a crease. Fold the strips in half again, lengthwise so that the folded edge covers the opposite side's raw edges.

Fold strips lengthwise and crease.

2. Steam press the strips when you complete them, and wrap them around a pincushion or scrap of batting. Secure the strips with pins.

Wrap prepared stems around batting.

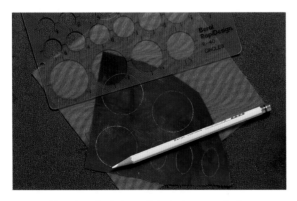

Sew the stem in place.

Preparing Circles

Place the appliqué fabric right side up on a sandpaper board. With a sharpened silver or white art pencil, trace the desired circle template onto the fabric, by drawing around the inside edge of the template. Cut out the fabric circle, adding a uniform, scant 1/8"-wide seam allowance. Set the circle aside, keeping it flat.

Use the circle template to trace a circle.

Preparing Freezer Paper Templates

In appliqué, the drawn line on a pattern is the sewing line. Transfer this line to the fabric using a template. Freezer-paper templates are easy to use and provide a place to write placement information.

1. Place the freezer paper shiny side down on the appliqué pattern. Use a mechanical pencil to trace each pattern piece. (Do not trace stems.) Leave space between each piece. Use a solid line to denote a stitched edge, and a dashed line to identify an edge that will be covered by an overlapping piece. Transfer all numbers from the patterns onto the templates as you trace them.

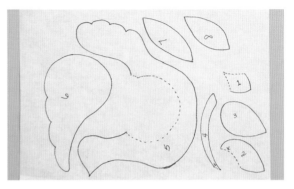

Transfer information from pattern to freezer paper.

2. Cut out each freezer-paper template on the solid line. Add an extra 1/8" along the dashed lines.

3. Match the templates to the fabrics you plan to use. Place the shiny side of the template on the right side of the fabric. Leave enough space between the pieces so that you can add an 1/8"-wide seam allowance to each fabric piece. Use a dry iron on the wool setting to press the freezer paper to the fabric. Press for about three seconds. Do not cut out the pieces yet.

4. Place the fabric/freezer paper layer right side up on your sandpaper board. Carefully trace around each template onto the fabric with a white or silver marking pencil. Trace only the solid lines. Carefully cut out each fabric piece, adding an 1/8"-wide seam allowance. Do not remove the freezer paper.

Place fabric and freezer paper right side up.

Placing Appliqués

Photocopy or trace the complete desired appliqué patterns onto unlined paper. Place the copied pattern on a lightbox, align the background fabric square (right side up) with the pattern, matching the fold lines. Pin the layers together.

Place stems on the background fabric first. Cut the required length of stem, plus a small amount extra. Insert a silk pin perpendicular to the stem, as shown.

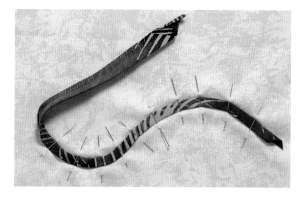

Insert pins perpendicular to the stems.

Work with a few prepared appliqué pieces at a time. Remove the freezer paper and position each piece on the background fabric following the numbered sequence indicated on the pattern. Pin the pieces in place and remove the block from the pattern. You are ready to baste the appliqués in place!

Pin appliqué pieces in place.

Basting

Use contrasting colored thread to baste your pinned pieces in place. Baste uniformly near the seamline for easy needle-turn appliqué.

For stems, thread your needle with a single strand of thread and knot the thread. Beginning from the front side, at the top of the stem, place a stitch on one side of the stem. Move across the stem to the opposite side, and take another stitch forward about $1/2$". Continue stitching back and forth across the stem. Place the stitches *just inside* the folded edge. From the top, the basting will appear as diagonal lines, but from the back the stitches will be straight and parallel to each other along both sides of the stems.

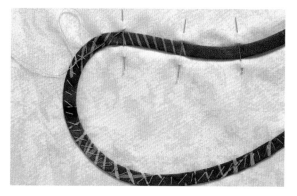

Basting stitch creates diagonal lines.

For circles, stitch an X tack, as shown, at least $1/8$" inside the seamlines. For larger circles, you may need a few more stitches.

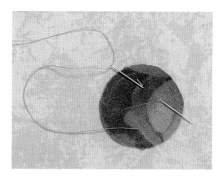

Basting a circle.

For all other shapes, baste at least ⅛" in from the seamline.

Baste all other shapes.

Needle-Turn Stitch

1. Thread the needle with a single 18" length of light-weight cotton thread in a color to match the appliqué fabric. Tie a knot in one end, leaving a ¼" tail.

2. Begin stitching the appliqué shape along a straight line rather than an inside or outside point. Roll the seam allowance under just until the drawn line disappears. Try to keep from rolling too much under the edge or the appliqué shape will be distorted. Use your thumb to lightly crease and hold the edge.

Use your thumb to crease and hold the edge.

3. Bring the needle up through both the background fabric and the folded edge of the appliqué, catching one or two threads along the fold. Pull the thread just taut enough, to avoid drawing up the fabric. Hide the tail under the appliqué so that the tail will not show from behind the background fabric. If you are right-handed, stitch from right to left, or counterclockwise. Reverse direction if you are left-handed.

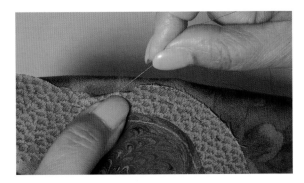

Catch one or two threads along the fold.

4. Insert the needle tip straight down into the background, where the thread came out of the folded edge of the appliqué. Slide the needle about ¹⁄₁₆" (two threads) along the underside of the background fabric, and come back up through the background and the folded edge, again catching one or two threads. When done correctly, the stitches will be hidden along the appliqué edge.

Work with your thumb and needle to manipulate and adjust the folded edge as you stitch. The sharp tip of the needle grips the outside edge of the seam allowance. Lift your thumb slightly while rolling under the allowance, then replace your thumb and hold the allowance in place. Push upward with the thumb to adjust the edge as you continue making stitches.

Use your thumb to hold the allowance in place.

5. When you finish stitching, or are nearly out of thread, insert the needle straight down into the background and pull the thread to the wrong side. Take two small stitches behind the appliqué, near the last stitch. Make a knot by bringing the needle through the last stitch. Weave the needle through a bit of background fabric behind the appliqué to anchor the tail. Trim the thread tail.

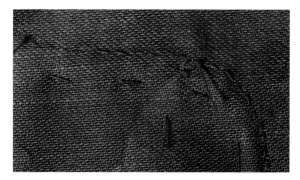

Take two small stitches behind the appliqué.

Make small, close stitches.

Stitching Stems

Some stems have another appliqué piece—such as a leaf—at their ends, which covers the raw edge of the stem. Other stems must be finished. To do this, stitch close to the end (about $3/4$") of the seam. Allow a $1/8$"-wide seam allowance, then trim the excess stem fabric. Fold under the seam allowance, using the tip of the needle, your finger, or thumb, and pin in place. Continue stitching toward the end of the stem, turn and stitch the short end, and finish by turning and stitching down the other side of the stem.

Outside Curves

Do not snip outside curves. Use the tip of your needle to ease the fabric along the edge of an outside curve as you sew. You may need to ease the fabric with every stitch, so keep your stitches small. A narrower seam allowance may be helpful, especially when appliquéing circles. When working on curves, do not prepare more than one stitch ahead. Think of it this way: ease—stitch, ease—stitch, and so on.

Stitching Circles

Be sure to maintain a scant $1/8$"seam allowance; do not clip the curves. Use the tip of the needle to roll under the seam allowance so the pencil line is not visible, and then pinch or finger-press the seamline for about $1/4$" to $1/2$". Moving forward from that creased area, roll under seam allowance, crease and stitch as for any outside curve.

Inside Curves

Clip inside curves just to the drawn seam line, never through it. You may need more clipping to make the tightest curves lie smoothly, but try to keep clips to a minimum. Clip at even intervals but in uneven numbers.

Move about 1" ahead of the area to be stitched and roll under the seam allowance. Use the side of the needle to turn under the edge of the appliqué and sweep it backward. Make small, close stitches.

Inside Points

1. When you are about three or four stitches from an inside point, stop and clip the seam allowance directly toward the V. Clip straight to the drawn line and then continue stitching up to the V with short stitches.

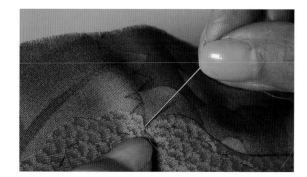

Use short stitches up to the V.

2. Make two or three $1/16$" satin stitches straight into the V, wrapping the thread around the tiny seam. Turn under the seam allowance on the other side of the V. Insert the needle in the last stitch and continue stitching away from the V, once again with short stitches.

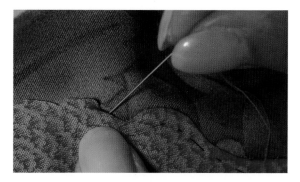

Continue with short stitches, away from the V.

Outside Points

1. Turn under the seam allowance and stitch toward the point. Continue stitching to within 1 or 2 threads of the marked point. Take a stay stitch right at the point, catching one thread of background and one thread of appliqué fabric. Trim, leaving at least $^1/_8$"-wide seam allowance. Gently pull the thread in the direction of the point, and pinch the point.

Bring the needle up at the point.

2. Use the tip of the needle to tuck under the point. Slip your thumbnail under the point to assist you. Take a second small stay stitch at the point, pulling the thread taut in the direction of the point, and pinching the point.

Tuck under the point with the needle.

3. Use the tip or the side of the needle to turn the seam allowance on the other side of the point. Place the tip of the needle in the last stitch at the point, and stitch down the second side.

Stitch down the second side.

Embroidery Stitches

Some appliqué patterns suggest embroidered embellishment such as a stem stitch or French knot.

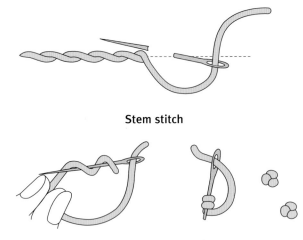

Stem stitch

French knot used for bird eyes

Pressing vs. Ironing

"Pressing" and "ironing" do not mean the same thing! Ironing involves moving the iron back and forth across the fabric. Pressing describes an up and down movement. Press, rather than iron appliqué work. For best results, place the appliquéd block face down on a firm surface covered with a dry terrycloth towel.

The Appliqué Patterns

A color photograph accompanies each pattern, with page references for techniques, tips, and suggestions. All appliqué pieces are numbered in the order in which they are stitched to the background square. Arrows indicate overlapping pieces. All blocks finish 8" square.

Prepare all background squares and the appliqué shapes following the instructions presented earlier in this chapter. Appliqué the design to the background square beginning with stems. Instructions for the needle-turn stitch begin on page 32.

Cutwork Patterns 1 & 2

Cutwork Pattern 1

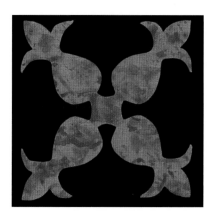

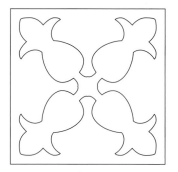

Cutwork Pattern 2

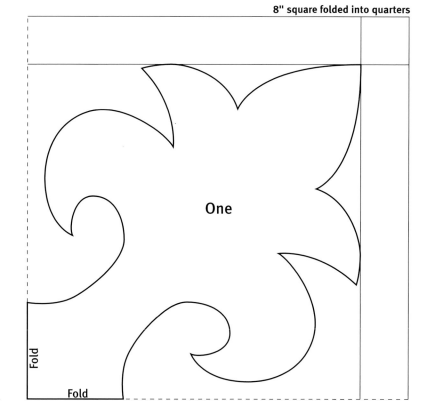

8" square folded into quarters

One

Fold

Fold

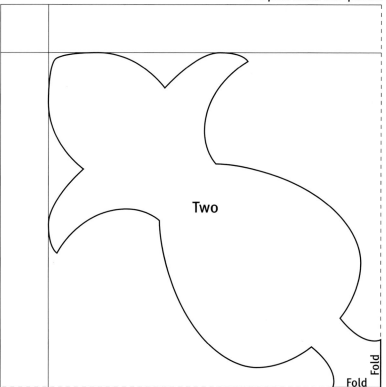

8" square folded into quarters

Two

Fold

Fold

APPLIQUÉ

CUTWORK PATTERNS 3 & 4

Cutwork Pattern 3

8" square folded into quarters

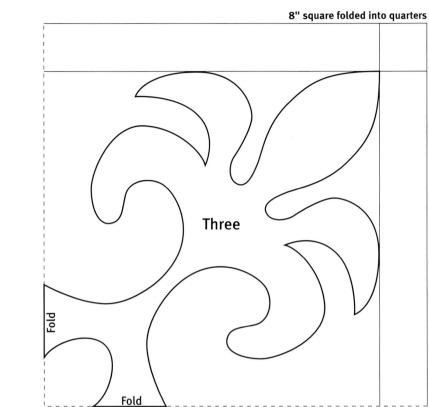

Three

Fold

Fold

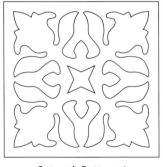

Cutwork Pattern 4

8" square folded into quarters

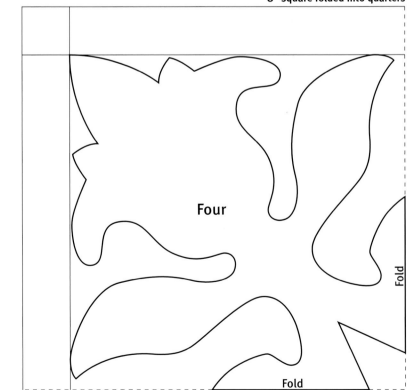

Four

Fold

Fold

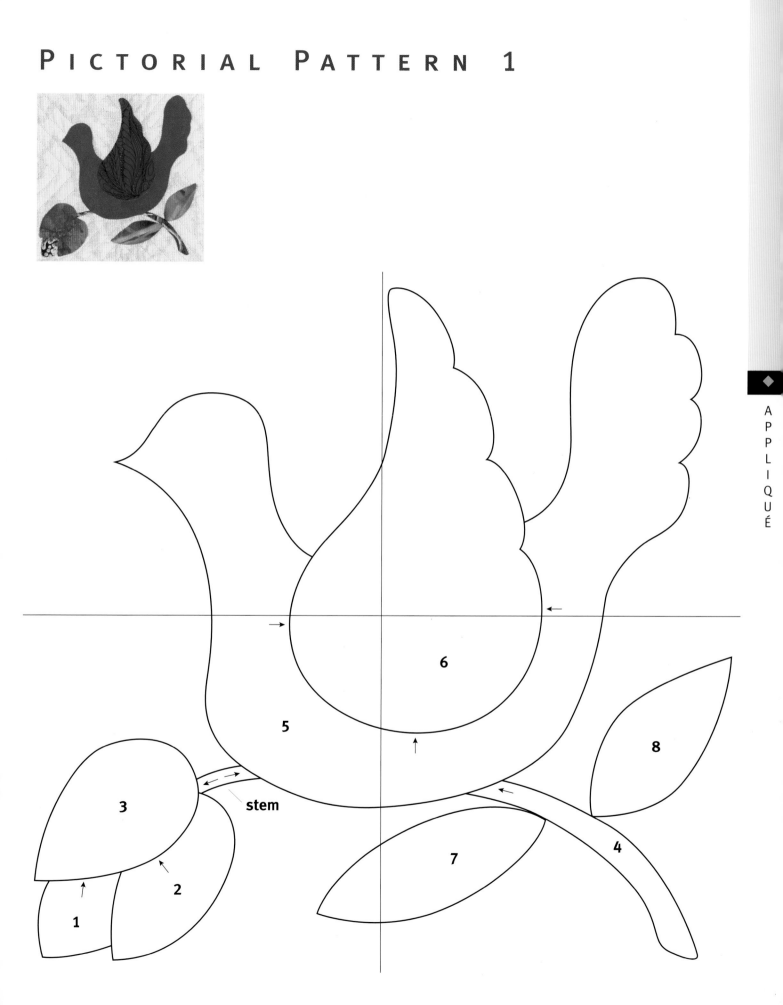

stem

1
2
3
4
5
6
7
8

PICTORIAL PATTERN 2

A P P L I Q U É

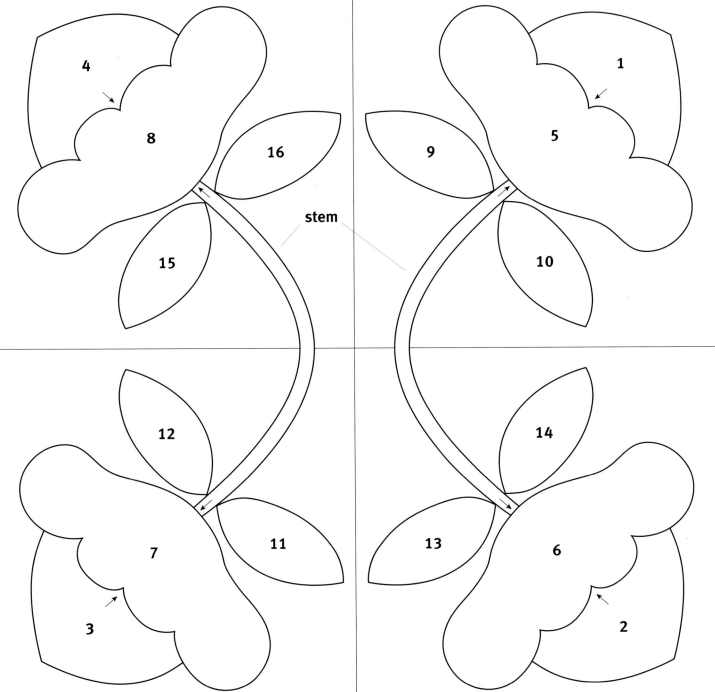

4

1

8

5

16

9

15

stem

10

12

14

7

11

13

6

3

2

PICTORIAL PATTERN 3

Appliqué the narrow stems and bird's leg to the background square, or embroider them, using a stem stitch (page 34). Refer to the instructions for narrow stems on pages 29–30.

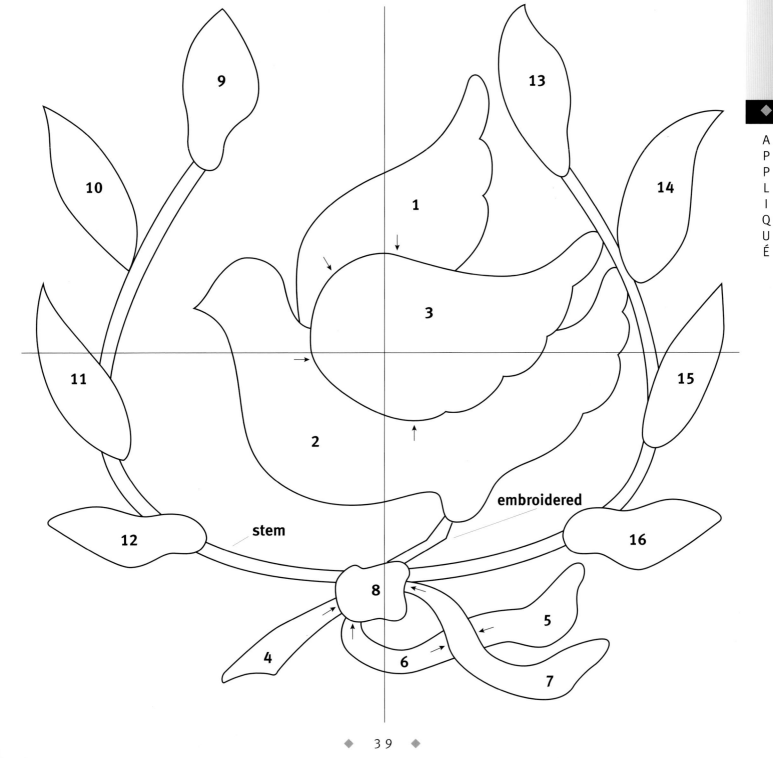

9

13

10

1

14

11

3

15

2

12

stem

embroidered

16

8

5

4

6

7

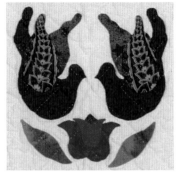

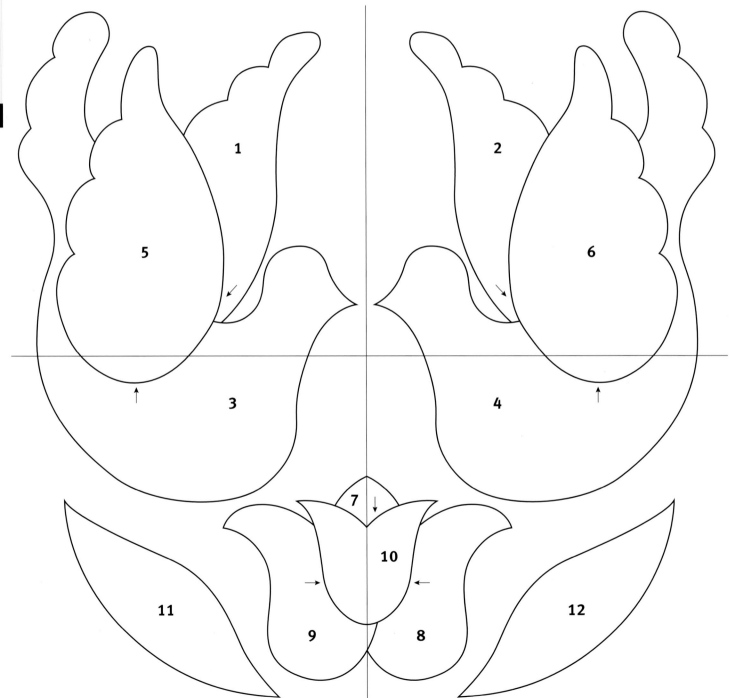

1

2

5

6

3

4

7

10

11

9

8

12

PICTORIAL PATTERN 5

The center of the star reveals the background fabric.

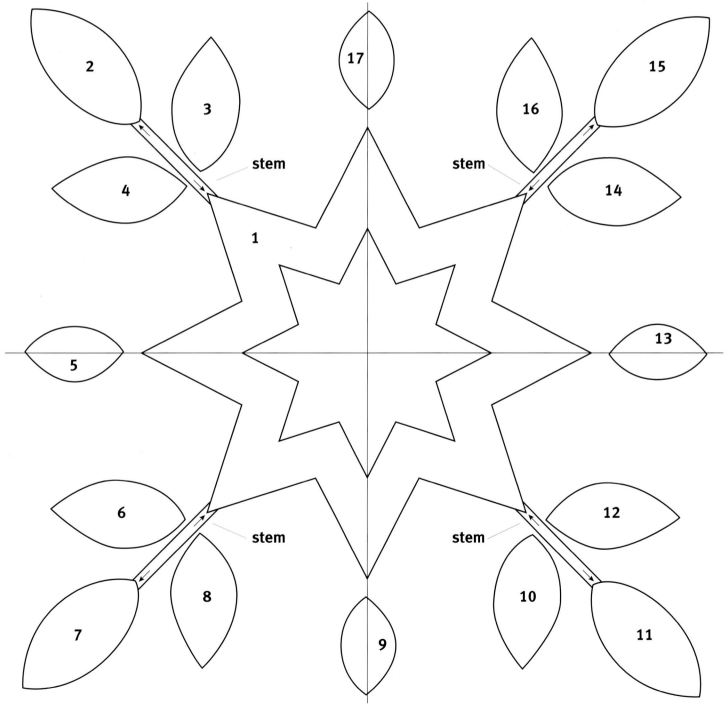

2

3

17

16

15

stem

stem

4

14

1

5

13

6

12

stem

stem

8

10

7

9

11

PICTORIAL PATTERN 6

The center of the star reveals the
background fabric.

PICTORIAL PATTERN 7

Make circles with a circle template. The short narrow stems are covered by the longer stems. Appliqué the stems, then the circles, before adding the remaining pieces.

PICTORIAL PATTERN 8

Make one leaf template and make circles with a circle template. The smaller stems are covered by the circular stem. Join raw edges of the circular stem. No appliqué order numbering needed.

PICTORIAL PATTERN 9

A circle of raw edge fabric is laid under the flower petals.

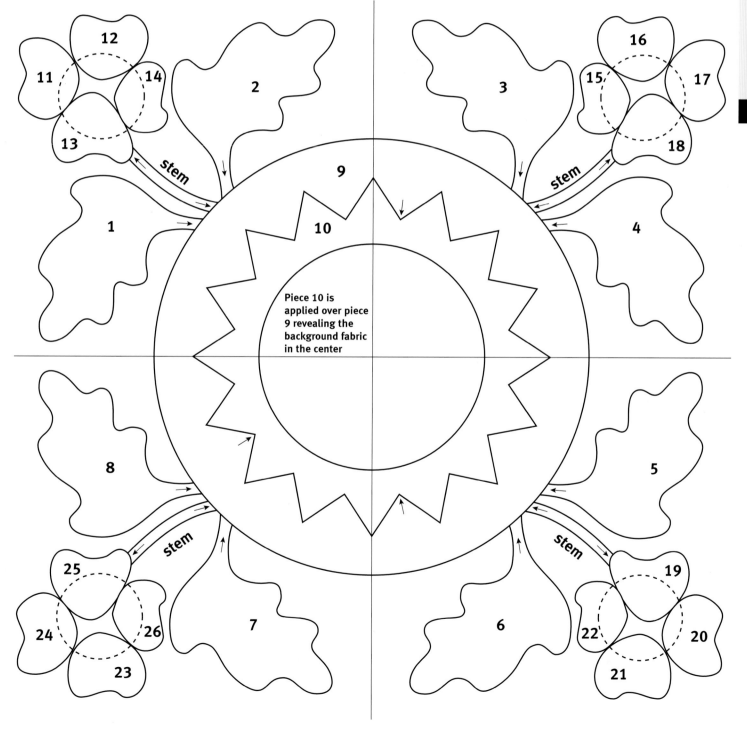

Piece 10 is applied over piece 9 revealing the background fabric in the center

PICTORIAL PATTERN 10

The center of Piece 1 reveals the background fabric. The two narrow stems can be embroidered using the stem stitch (page 34). Appliqué the two wider stems to the background.

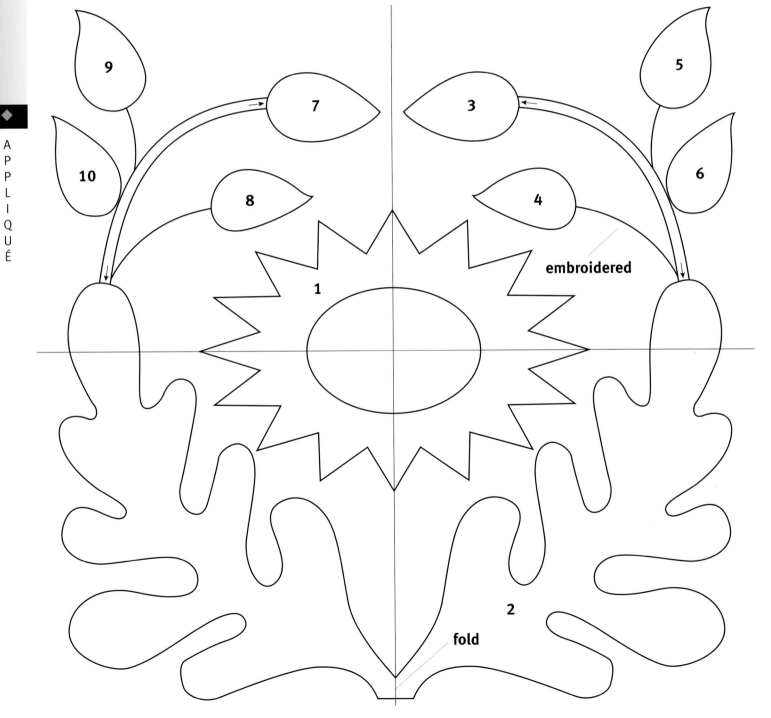

embroidered

fold

PICTORIAL PATTERN 11

The stems to Pieces 11 and 14 are placed before the stems leading to Pieces 13 and 16.

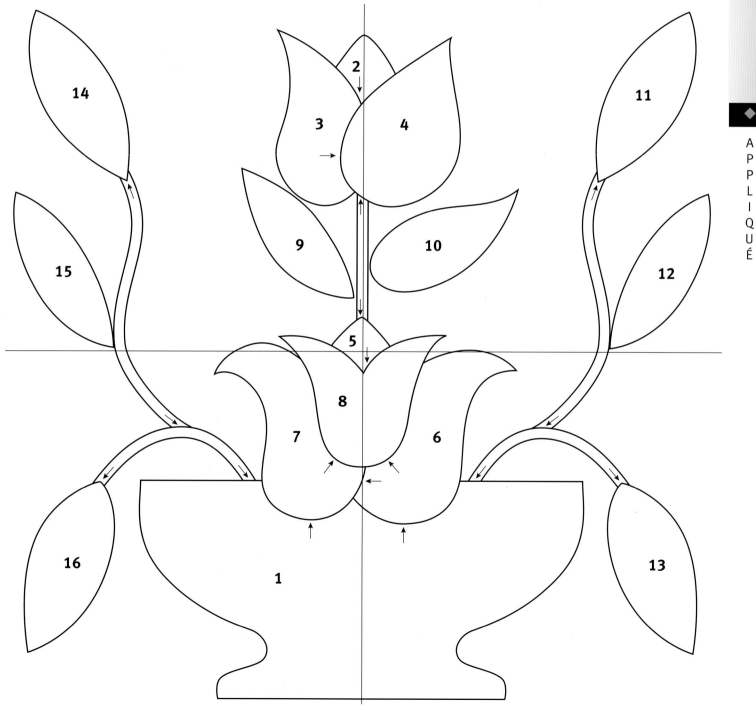

PICTORIAL PATTERN 12

APPLIQUÉ

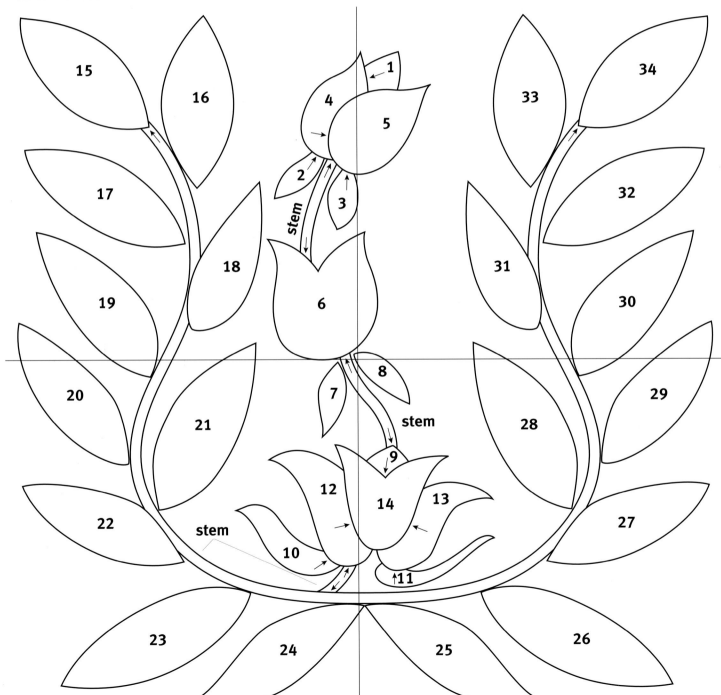

15

16

1

4

5

2

3

stem

6

17

18

19

31

32

33

34

30

20

7

8

stem

21

28

29

9

12

14

13

22

stem

10

11

27

28

23

24

25

26

PICTORIAL PATTERN 13

Weave the basket, using prepared stems.
Appliqué the stems to the background square.
The side stems and Pieces 15, 16, 17, and 18
cover the raw edges.

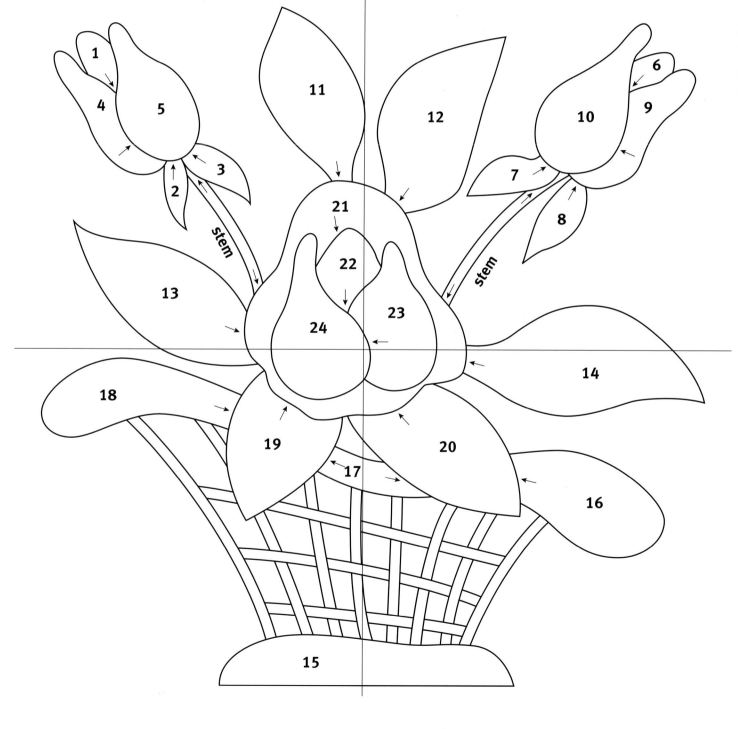

PICTORIAL PATTERN 14

The unnumbered tree parts are stems.

**The First Spring of the
New Millenium**

Pieced by Sally Coble,
machine quiled by Linda Walsh

66" x 66"

Midnight Madness

Pieced and quilted by Patsy Biggs

67" x 67"

A Few of My Favorite Things

Pieced and quilted by Nancy Farmer

62" x 62"

PATCHWORK

Patchwork blocks provide endless design possibilities.

Akey advantage to hand piecing is that, like hand appliqué, it is portable. There are many places where stitching makes the time go faster—flying on airplanes and riding on trains among others.

In this chapter, I provide instructions for making and using templates, and for piecing by hand (including curves!). Use the techniques to make the Evening Star blocks (pages 60–73), Eight-Pointed Star blocks (pages 74–80), and Mariner's Compass blocks (pages 81–85).

Some pieced patterns in this book include rotary cutting conversions. Any of the pieced blocks can be assembled by machine. If you have never tried cutting without templates and piecing by machine, you can practice the technique by making an Evening Star block. Try all the techniques and decide which you enjoy the most.

KEYS TO SUCCESS!

Fresh, fine needles and pins glide through the fabric easily.
Use short (18") lengths of thread to prevent tangles.
To minimize thread tangles and preserve the finish on your needles, always stitch with clean hands.
Work with a sharp rotary blade.
Keep your machine is in good working order.
Good lighting is essential!

Template Method: Seamline

This method transfers the seamline to the wrong side of the fabric pieces. After the seamlines are marked, you will add the seam allowances as you cut the fabric. Photocopy or trace the pattern pieces from the book. If you copy them, measure the pieces, because sometimes photocopying may distort the images.

1. Place the photocopy on your cutting mat. Use removable tape to tape a sheet of plastic template material over the pattern pieces. Place a cutting ruler along one side of each pattern piece, aligning the edge of the ruler with the center of the pattern line. Use a wallpaper or box knife or a rotary cutter with a recycled blade to cut out the template. If you use a wallpaper knife, stroke slightly against the ruler to score, and snap the plastic.

Apply pressure down and toward the ruler.

2. Place the template on the pattern to confirm its accuracy. You should just be able to see the printed line of the pattern along the edge. At the same time, use a fine-tip permanent marker to mark the identification letters and straight-grain arrow. Do not trace the pattern lines onto the template.

3. Smooth the fabric face down on a sandpaper board. Place the template on top of the fabric, and use a mechanical pencil (or a silver or white marking pencil) to mark around the outside edge of the template. Leave at least $^1/_2$" between the pieces so you will have enough fabric to add seam allowances when cutting each piece. Repeat with all pattern pieces as indicated on the block. Cut out the pieces, adding a $^1/_4$"-wide seam allowance with scissors, or use a rotary cutter and ruler. Lay the $^1/_4$" marking on the drawn line and add an accurate $^1/_4$"-wide seam allowance as you cut. Or use a pre-made template for patchwork. Refer to Resources (page 110) for ordering information.

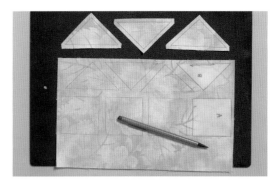

Leave at least $^1/_2$" between pieces.

Template Method: Cut Line

This method uses the cut line as the guide for stitching, while still providing a guide at seamline intersections. If you prefer the speed of rotary cut pieces, but would like the assistance of templates for accuracy or fussy cutting, make templates that include $^1/_4$" seam allowances. With the plastic over the pattern piece, make a small dot at any intersection points with a permanent marker. At each dot, use a $^1/_{16}$" hole punch to make a hole. Place the template over the cut fabric pieces and mark the intersections with a pencil.

Fussy Cutting

You can create awesome effects by selectively cutting identical shapes from repeat fabric motifs. This is called "fussy cutting." Be aware that this technique often requires more fabric, depending on the pattern repeat. The results, however, are definitely worth it!

Templates make it easy to fussy cut fabrics. Study the fabric and move the template around the surface, isolating various motifs. Trace a common feature of the desired motif onto your template with a pencil. Match the marks on the template to the fabric to cut the required number of pieces.

Piecing by Hand

Each block pattern provides assembly instructions. Seam allowances are left free, and can be pressed in any direction.

1. Lay out the entire block, placing the pieces right side up.

2. Refer to the piecing sequence, and place the first two pieces right sides together. Insert a silk pin, front to back, into the point where two pencil lines intersect, at the beginning of the seamline facing you. Turn the two pieces over to make sure that the sewing lines are perfectly aligned. Adjust by repinning as needed. Be certain that the pieces do not shift as you pin. Repeat at the other end of the seamline. For longer seams, you may want to add another pin at the midpoint. Always verify that the pins fall on the seamlines.

Insert a pin into the intersection.

3. Thread a #11 Appliqué Sharp needle with an 18"-long single strand of thread (50/3 cotton) in a color that blends with your fabrics. Working from the top side, insert the tip of the needle at the first pin on the sewing line. Pull the stitch through, approximately ¼" from the knot. Take another stitch in the same place, and pull the thread taut. This secures the starting point while keeping the bulk of a knot away. Remove the pin.

KEYS TO SUCCESS!

As you stitch, clip the end of the thread when it develops a "split end." This prevents tangles and allows the thread to glide smoothly through fabric.

4. Holding the fabric taut, stitch along the seamline, taking a few stitches at a time on the needle. Check underneath to make sure that the stitches are exactly on the seamline. Pull the needle and thread through the fabric, smoothing the stitches.

5. Insert the needle again, just behind the last stitch to create a backstitch. This strengthens the line of stitching. Continue stitching along the seamline, removing pins as you approach them. When you reach the last pin, back out the head of the pin, but keep the tip in place until you pull the final stitch through the exact end of the marked seamline. Take one more stitch through that point and, before pulling the loop closed, slip the needle through the loop and pull gently to knot.

Start stitching at the intersection.
Remove pins as you stitch toward them.

6. When you reach an intersection where seams join, stitch to the exact end of the seamline, and then pass the needle through the seam allowance to the start of the seam allowance on the adjoining piece. Double stitch both before and after the seam and continue stitching as described in Steps 4 and 5. The seam allowances are free to be pressed in either direction.

Keep seam allowance free.

Hand Piecing Curves

Hand piecing curves is easier than it looks. Try this technique by making the Sunflower pattern (page 82), which is a variation of the Mariner's Compass.

1. Use the tip of a wallpaper knife to make *closely spaced* perforations along the curved edge of the plastic template. Use paper scissors to cut out the template, along the perforated line. Transfer the degree lines from the pattern to the template.

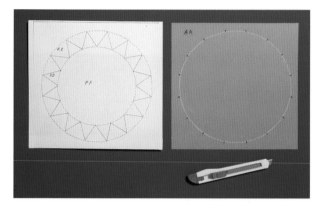

Transfer degree lines to the template.

2. Place the template on the wrong side of the fabric and mark the sewing lines. Transfer the degree line information to the fabric with small dashes. Cut out the fabric shape, adding a $1/4$"–wide seam allowance. The degree lines provide a guide to align and stitch the curved edges smoothly in place.

Transfer degree lines to the fabric.

3. Pin carefully and generously, and check the underside seam allowance often as you stitch. Sew with the concave curve on top. Press seams toward the convex curve.

Piecing by Machine

Try this technique by making one Evening Star block (page 66) without templates, using your favorite rotary cutting method.

Stitching an exact $1/4$"-wide seam allowance is key to accurate machine piecing. A machine presser foot that measures $1/4$" from the needle to the outside right edge of the foot is ideal. To test your machine for seam-width accuracy, stitch a seam, and then measure the seam allowance. If the measurement is not exactly $1/4$", place a ruler under the presser foot and slowly drop the needle until it touches the $1/4$" line on the ruler. Place several layers of masking tape along the edge of the ruler. If the $1/4$" mark falls under the presser foot, cut a small notch in the tape so it does not interfere with the presser foot or the machine's feed dogs.

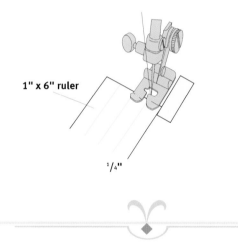

1" x 6" ruler

$1/4$"

KEYS TO SUCCESS!

When machine piecing, cut pieces to include $1/4$"-wide seam allowance.

Stitch seams, raw edge to raw edge.

Press seams to one side, toward darker fabric when possible.

Never Say Never
Pieced by Fran Snay,
hand quilted by Eddy Branch
63" x 63"

Red is Cool
Pieced and quilted
by Anna Fell
47" x 47"

A Graceful Waiting

Pieced by Barbara Pipes,
machine quilted by Sue Champion

46 $^1/_2$" x 57"

EVENING STAR

Stunning combinations result by varying the classic Evening Star block.

Before beginning, review Fabric Selection (page 18) and read through the fabric suggestions for each Evening Star variation. Study the quilts throughout the book, paying special attention to how each quiltmaker used various fabrics to achieve her unique look.

Refer to Patchwork (page 54) for making templates, cutting fabric, and stitching techniques. These blocks are easily assembled using machine-piecing techniques.

The instructions are for one 8" (finished) block.

Note: Variations One through Six feature different 4" (finished) pieced center squares, which replace piece K in the 8" Evening Star block. Variations Seven through Fifteen feature nine different 4" finished appliquéd center squares, also to replace piece K. Use them in combination with any of the pieced and appliqué blocks, or set them together as seen in my quilt Dawn's Influence *(page 73).*

Variation Sixteen is a 8" (finished) block called Devil's Claw. Assembly instructions for each variation are included.

Evening Star

Fabric Suggestions

Use a favorite large-scale print for piece K (center square) and fabrics that contrast clearly with the background fabric for piece I (star points).

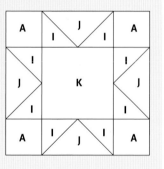

Cutting

Patterns are on page 67.
Template I: Cut 8 from contrasting fabric (star points).
Template J: Cut 4 from the background fabric.
Template A: Cut 4 from the background fabric.
Template K: Cut 1 from a large-scale print fabric.

See Alternate Rotary Method on page 66.

Assembly

Complete the block as shown.

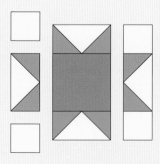

Variation One

Fabric Suggestions

A border print is a great choice here; it will outline the square and create a unique center design. Orient the long side of template J (triangle) with the straight grain of the print.

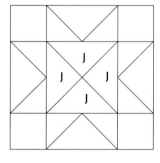

Cutting

Patterns are on page 67.
Cutting instructions are for a 4" (finished) center.
Template J: Cut 4 from a striped or other directional fabric.

Alternate Rotary Method

Cut 1 square 5 1/4" x 5 1/4" from 2 different fabrics. Then cut each square twice diagonally. Use 2 triangles from each fabric to create the center square.

Assembly

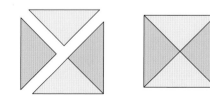

Variation Two

Fabric Suggestions

Orient the long side of template I on a directional print fabric. To outline the center square, use a large-scale print fabric for piece FF (center square). *Note: Normally, straight grain will be on the outside edges of these pieces, but in this case, let the fabric design dictate the cut.*

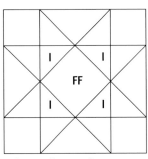

Cutting

Patterns are on pages 67–68.
Cutting instructions are for a 4" (finished) center square.
Template I: Cut 4 from a directional print.
Template FF: Cut 1 from a large-scale print.

Alternate Rotary Method

Piece FF: Cut 1 square $3^{1}/_{8}$" x $3^{1}/_{8}$" from a large-scale print.
Piece I: Cut 2 squares $2^{7}/_{8}$" x $2^{7}/_{8}$" from a directional print. Cut each square once diagonally.

Assembly

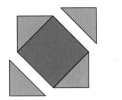

Variation Three

Fabric Suggestions

Use multiple fabrics to achieve a scrappy look. Fussy cut (page 55) 4 flowers and sew 4 triangles together for a stunning design.

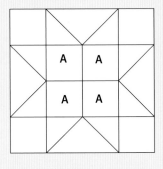

Cutting

Patterns are on page 67.
Cutting instructions are for a 4" (finished) center.
Template A: Cut 4 from 4 different fabrics, or fussy cut from 1 fabric.

Alternate Rotary Method

Cut 1 square each $2^{1}/_{2}$" x $2^{1}/_{2}$", from 4 different fabrics or fussy cut 4 squares from 1 fabric.

Assembly

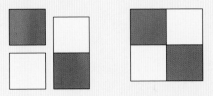

Variation Four

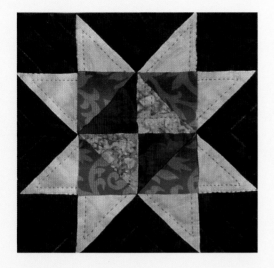

Fabric Suggestions

Create an interesting center by aligning the long sides of the 4 triangles with a directional print fabric, or fussy cutting the triangles from a large-scale floral print. For a scrappy look, use assorted fabrics.

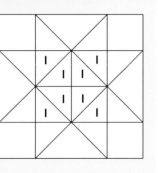

Cutting

Patterns are on page 67.
Cutting instructions are for a 4" (finished) center.
Template I: Cut 8 from assorted fabrics.

Alternate Rotary Method

Cut 4 squares $2^7/_8$" x $2^7/_8$" from assorted fabrics. Cut each square once diagonally.

Assembly

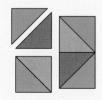

Variation Five

Fabric Suggestions

Feature a favorite print in the center square (piece L), framed by a directional print (piece M).

Cutting

Patterns are on page 67.
Cutting instructions are for a 4" (finished) center.
Template M: Cut 4 from a directional print fabric.
Template L: Cut 1 from a favorite print fabric.

Alternate Rotary Method

Piece M: Cut 4 rectangles 1" x $5^1/_4$". Cut ends at a 45° angle in opposite directions.
Piece L: Cut 1 square $3^1/_2$" x $3^1/_2$".

Assembly

Sew a M to opposite sides of L.

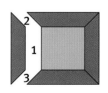

Sew remaining M's to L seams first, then sew M seams together.

Variation Six

Fabric Suggestions

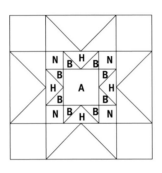

A 4" (finished) Evening Star becomes the center of an 8" (finished) Evening Star block. Use the same fabric for piece B (star points), and the same background fabric used in the larger star for pieces H and N. Vary the look by creating the center star from totally different fabrics.

Cutting

Patterns are on page 67.

Cutting instructions are for a 4" (finished) center.
Template A: Cut 1 from your assorted fabrics.
Template B: Cut 8 from your assorted fabrics.
Template H: Cut 4 from the background fabric.
Template N: Cut 4 from the background fabric.

Alternate Rotary Method

Piece A: Cut 1 square 2 1/2" x 2 1/2".
Piece B: Cut 8 squares 1 1/2" x 1 1/2".
Piece H: Cut 4 rectangles 1 1/2" x 2 1/2".
Piece N: Cut 4 squares 1 1/2" x 1 1/2".

Assembly

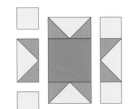

Make 4

Variation Seven–Fifteen

Cutting

Patterns are on pages 67 and 68–72.
Template K: Cut 1 background square for each variation. Prepare and cut the appropriate appliqué patterns as described on pages 29–30.

Alternate Rotary Method

Piece K: Cut 1 background square 4 1/2" x 4 1/2" for each variation.

Assembly

Appliqué the center motif prior to piecing the block. Refer to the assembly instructions for the Evening Star (page 61).

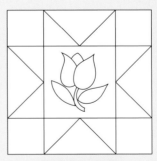

Variation Seven

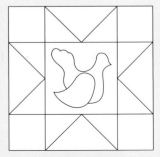

Variation Eight

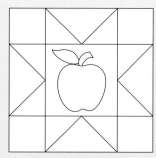

Variation Nine

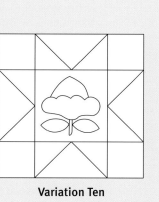

Variation Ten

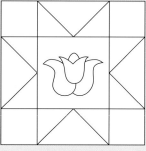

Variation Eleven

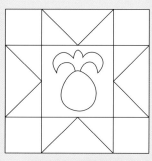

Variation Twelve

Variation Thirteen

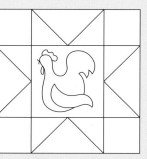

Variation Fourteen

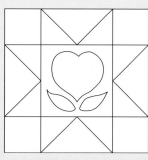

Variation Fifteen

Variation Sixteen "Devil's Claw"

Fabric Suggestions

Add interest to your quilt with this block by mixing a variety of fabrics in this final variation. Work completely scrappy, or with limited combinations of backgrounds and other block fabrics.

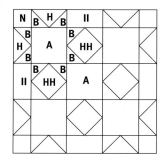

Cutting

Patterns are on page 67.

Cutting instructions are for one 8" (finished) block.

Template B: Cut 32 from fabric 1 (star points).

Template H: Cut 8 from the background fabric.

Template HH: Cut 4 from the background fabric.

Template A: Cut 4 from fabric 2 (another fabric of your choice). Cut 1 from the background fabric.

Template II: Cut 4 from the background fabric.

Template N: Cut 4 from the background fabric.

See Alternate Rotary Method on page 66.

Assembly

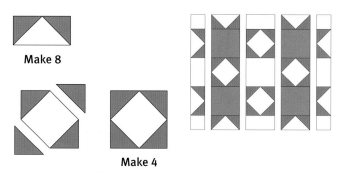

Make 8

Make 4

Evening Star
(continued)

Alternate Rotary Method

Piece I: Cut 8 squares 2 ½" x 2 ½" from a contrasting fabric (star points).

Piece J: Cut 4 rectangles 2 ½" x 4 ½" from the background fabric.

Piece A: Cut 4 squares 2 ½" x 2 ½" from the background fabric.

Piece K: Cut 1 square 4 ½" x 4 ½" from a printed fabric (or the background fabric, if you plan to add appliqué to the star center).

Assembly

For rotary cut pieces, use a pencil and ruler to draw a diagonal line from one corner to the opposite corner on each I square. Sew two I squares to a J rectangle as shown. Trim the excess fabric from the I squares only.

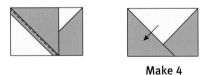

Make 4

Refer to block assembly on page 61.

Variation Sixteen "Devil's Claw"
(continued)

Alternate Rotary Method

Piece B: Cut 32 squares 1 ½" x 1 ½" from fabric 1 (star points).

Pieces H and II: Cut 12 rectangles 1 ½" x 2 ½" from the background fabric.

Piece HH: Cut 4 squares 2" x 2" from background fabric.

Piece A: Cut 4 squares 2 ½" x 2 ½" from fabric 2. Cut 1 square 2 ½" x 2 ½" from the background fabric.

Piece N: Cut 4 squares 1 ½" x 1 ½" from the background fabric.

Refer to block assembly on page 65.

EVENING STAR PATTERNS

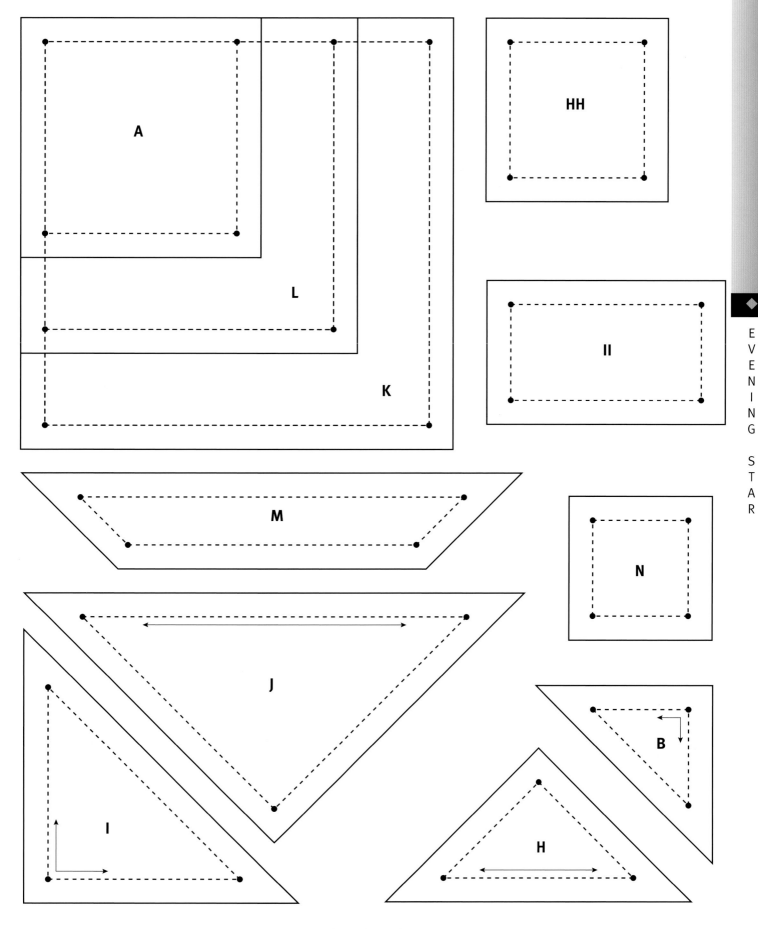

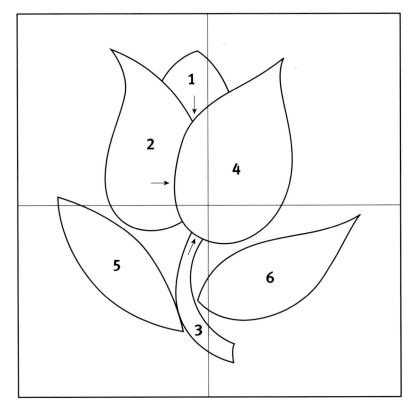

Variation Seven

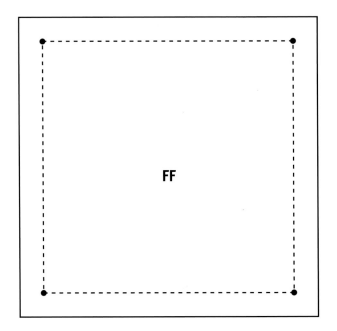

FF

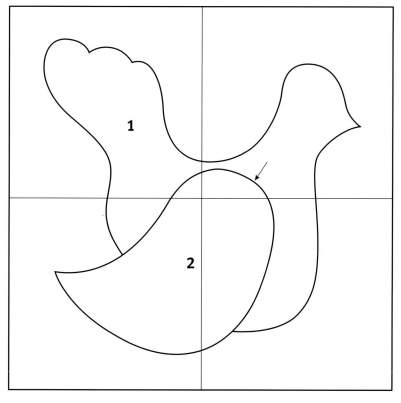

Variation Eight

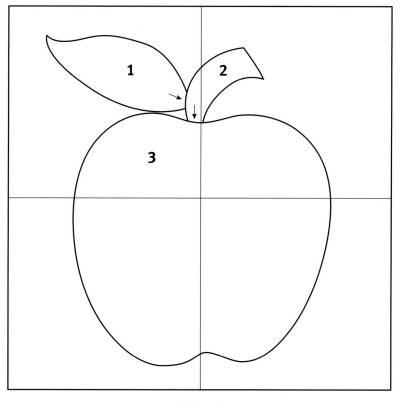

Variation Nine

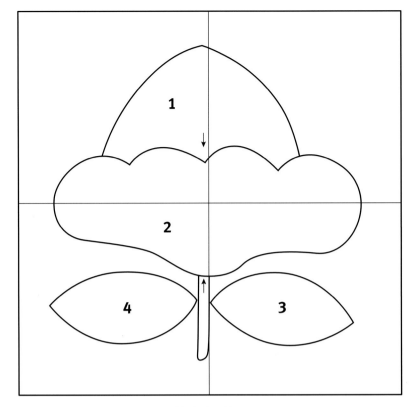

Variation Ten

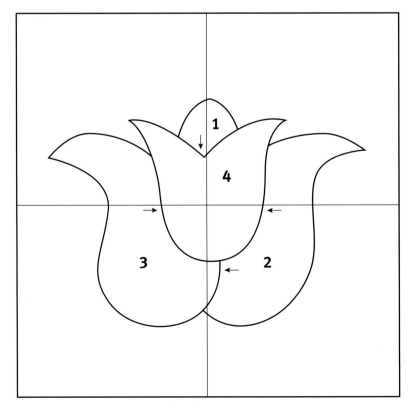

Variation Eleven

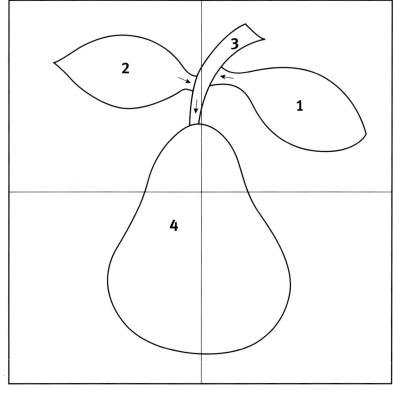

Variation Twelve

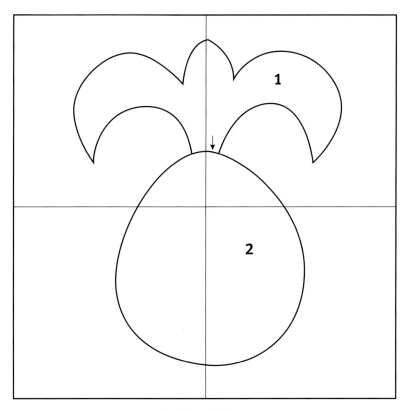

Variation Thirteen

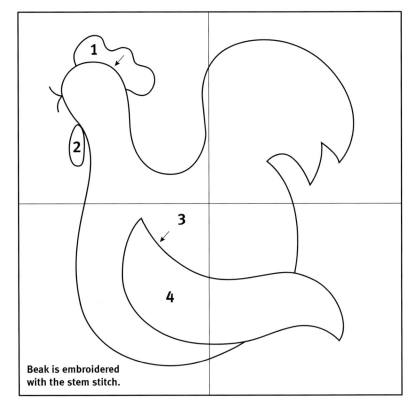

Beak is embroidered
with the stem stitch.

Variation Fourteen

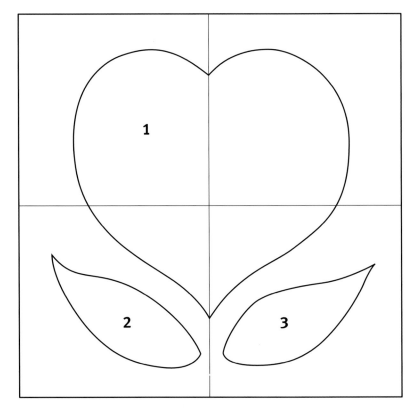

Variation Fifteen

Dawn's Influence
Hand pieced and hand quilted
by Darlene Christopherson
48" x 48"

6 EIGHT-POINTED STAR

Use directional print fabrics to make an awesome Eight-Pointed Star block.

This traditional pattern is composed of eight diamonds, four triangles, and four squares. Each variation incorporates minor changes to these shapes, and to the placement of colors and values, to achieve different visual effects.

Before beginning, review Fabric Selection (page 18) and read the fabric suggestions for each Eight-Pointed Star variation. Study the quilts throughout the book, paying special attention to how each quiltmaker used fabrics to achieve her unique look.

Refer to Patchwork (page 54) for making templates, cutting fabric, and stitching techniques. These blocks are easily assembled using hand- or machine-piecing techniques.

Instructions are for one 8" (finished) block.

Note: Variations Two through Five use piece U in the four corners and piece P on the four sides of the block. You can substitute pieced corner squares, made with piece P, as in Variation One.

Eight-Pointed Star

Fabric Suggestions

Consider fussy cutting fabric (page 55) for piece O. Use directional print fabrics, including appropriate border prints, to create awesome radiating effects, or to give the illusion of a wreath within the star.

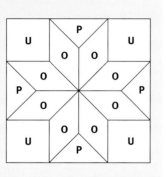

Cutting

Patterns are on page 78.
Fabric 1, 2, and so on refer to a fabric of your choice.
Template O: Cut 8 from fabric 1.
Template P: Cut 4 from fabric 2.
Template U: Cut 4 from fabric 3.

Alternate Rotary Method
Piece O: Cut 1 strip $2\frac{1}{8}$" x 40" from fabric 1. Cut eight 45° diamonds, each $2\frac{1}{8}$".
Piece P: Cut 1 square $4\frac{1}{2}$" x $4\frac{1}{2}$" from fabric 2. Cut the square twice diagonally to make 4 triangles.
Piece U: Cut 4 squares $2\frac{7}{8}$" x $2\frac{7}{8}$" from fabric 3.
Mark a dot at seamline intersections.

Assembly

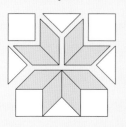

Many seam allowances meet at the center. Pin and double stitch at the intersection.

Variation One

Fabric Suggestions

This variation splits the corner squares into triangles, creating the illusion of an octagon surrounding the star. Orient the long side of piece P with a striped or other directional print.

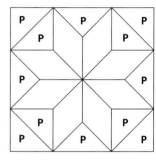

Cutting

Patterns are on page 78.
Template P: Cut 4 from background fabric. Cut 8 from a striped or directional print.

Alternate Rotary Method
Piece P: Cut 2 squares $3\frac{1}{4}$" x $3\frac{1}{4}$" from the background fabric. Cut each square once diagonally.
Cut 2 squares $4\frac{1}{2}$" x $4\frac{1}{2}$" from contrasting fabric. Cut squares twice diagonally.
Mark dot at seam intersections.

Assembly

Make 4

Variation Two

Fabric Suggestions

To outline the centermost star, cut pieces R and Rr from a striped or other directional print fabric, or from a sharply contrasting fabric. Try a geometric print or one that features flowers in a row.

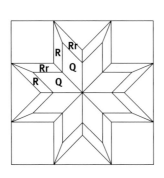

Cutting

Patterns are on page 78.
Cutting instructions are for the diamonds.
Template R and Rr: Cut 8 each from directional print fabric.
Template Q: Cut 8 from fabric 1.

Assembly

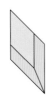

Make 8

Variation Three

Fabric Suggestions

Piece S (star center) can create an octagon or an interlocking design. Use two values for pieces T and Tr to create a beveled effect.

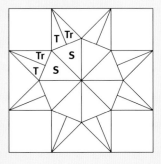

Cutting

Patterns are on page 78.
Cutting instructions are for the diamonds.
Template T: Cut 8 from fabric 1.
Template Tr: Cut 8 from fabric 2.
Template S: Cut 8 from fabric 3.

Assembly

Make 8

Variation Four

Fabric Suggestions

As with Variation Three, create an octagon by selecting two different directional print fabrics for piece S. Orient the short side of piece S with the direction of the print. You can separate the two pieces by either color or value.

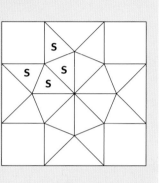

Cutting

Patterns are on page 78.
Cutting instructions are for the diamonds.
Template S: Cut 8 from fabric 1. Cut 8 from fabric 2.

Assembly

Make 8

Variation Five

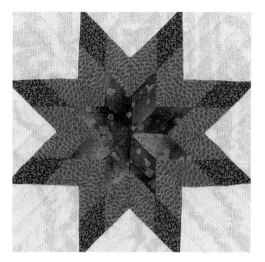

Fabric Suggestions

Four smaller V diamonds are sewn together to create the larger diamond, replacing piece O in the basic Eight-Pointed Star design.

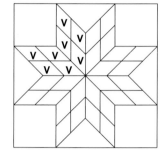

Cutting

Patterns are on page 78.
Cutting instructions are for the diamonds.
Template V: Cut 8 from fabric 1. Cut 16 from fabric 2. Cut 8 from fabric 3.

Alternate Rotary Method

Piece V: Cut 1 strip $1^{5}/_{16}$" x 21" from fabric 1. Cut eight 45° diamonds $1^{5}/_{16}$". Cut 1 strip $1^{5}/_{16}$" x 42" from fabric 2. Cut sixteen 45° diamonds $1^{5}/_{16}$". Cut 1 strip $1^{5}/_{16}$" x 21" from fabric 3. Cut eight 45° diamonds $1^{5}/_{16}$". Mark a dot at seam intersections.

Assembly

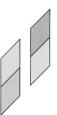 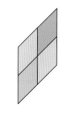

Make 8

EIGHT-POINTED STAR PATTERNS

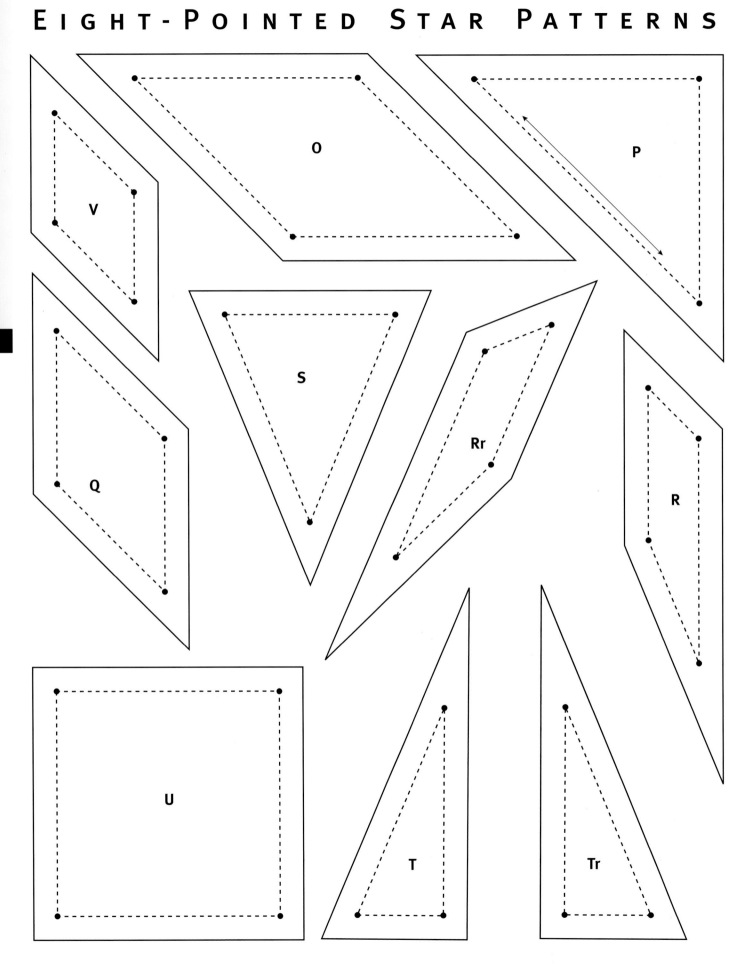

My Perfect Union
Pieced and quilted
by Shirley Pinkston
$58^1/_2$" x $58^1/_2$"

A Whimsical Christmas
Pieced and quilted
by Michelle Weller
44" x 44"

Encompassing Sunflowers

Hand pieced by
Darlene Christopherson,
machine quilted
by Julie Zentell

60" x 60"

MARINER'S COMPASS

Choice of fabric enhances the graphic qualities of the Mariner's Compass block.

Before beginning, review Fabric Selection (page 18), and read the fabric suggestions for each Mariner's Compass variation. Study the quilts throughout the book, paying special attention to how each quiltmaker used fabrics to achieve her unique look. Refer to Patchwork (page 54) for making templates, cutting fabric, and stitching techniques.

Instructions are for one 8" (finished) block.

KEYS TO SUCCESS!

These patterns must be cut with templates.
Be sure to mark all registration lines on the templates!

Octagon Compass

Fabric Suggestions

Use a background fabric that contrasts with the compass points for piece AA. Use either the background or any other fabric for piece Z. To create a radiating look select a directional print for either Y or X. If you wish, you can fussy cut (page 55) any of the pieces. Cut piece W from a favorite large-scale print or from fabric appropriate for a signature block.

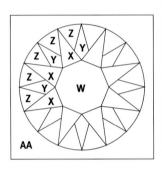

Cutting

Patterns are on pages 84–85.
Template Z: Cut 16 from the background fabric.
Template Y: Cut 8 from a directional print.
Template X: Cut 8 from a directional fabric.
Template W: Cut 1 from a large-scale print.
Template AA: Cut 1 from the background fabric.

Assembly

Step 1: Make 8   **Step 2: Make 4**

3. Sew X/Y/Z units to remaining 4 piece X's to complete the compass ring.

Assembly continued on page 83.

Sunflower

Fabric Suggestions

Traditionally, Sunflower points contrast well with the background fabric. The large center is a perfect place to feature a signature block, a large-scale print, or to show off fancy quilting. You might also select one of the appliqué variations shown on pages 68–72.

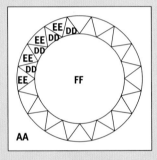

Cutting

Patterns are on pages 84–85.
Template DD: Cut 16 from a contrasting fabric.
Template EE: Cut 16 from the background fabric.
Template FF: Cut 1 from a large-scale print fabric, appliqué background, or fabric for a signature block.
Template AA: Cut 1 from the background fabric.

Assembly

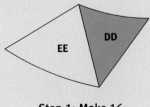

Step 1: Make 16

2. Sew DD/EE units together to create a ring.

Assembly continued on page 83.

Sunflower and Star

Fabric Suggestions

To accentuate the graphic qualities of this block, use contrasting fabrics for piece DD. For additional inspiration, refer to Fussy Cutting (page 55) and to the fabric suggestions for making Eight-Pointed Stars (page 74).

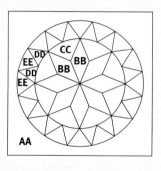

Cutting

Patterns are on pages 84–85.
Fabrics 1, 2, and so on refer to a fabric of your choice.
Template BB: Cut 4 each from fabrics 1 and 2.
Template CC: Cut 8 from fabric 3 or background fabric.
Template DD: Cut 16 from fabric 4.
Template EE: Cut 16 from the background fabric.
Template AA: Cut 1 from the background fabric.

Assembly

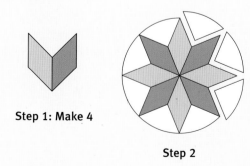

Step 1: Make 4

Step 2

Assembly continued on the right.

Octagon Compass assembly continued:

4. Sew piece W to the inside of the ring. With right sides together, match, pin, and sew one octagon side to piece X. Repeat to complete the compass.

5. With right sides together, sew the center compass to the inside of piece AA. Refer to Hand Piecing Curves (page 57) as needed. Match the seamline and dashed (degree) lines marked on piece AA to the marked seamlines of each piece Z. Align the degree lines to the intersection points of the X and Y pieces. Pin and sew *one* piece Z at a time.

Sunflower assembly continued:

3. Match piece FF degree marks with the points of EE and pin. Sew piece FF (center circle) to the inside of the DD/EE ring. Use the marked seamlines on both pieces assist with alignment. Refer to Hand Piecing Curves (page 57) as needed.

4. Refer to Octagon Compass, Step 5 (above) as needed to complete the block. Match degree lines to points of DD.

Sunflower and Star assembly continued:

3. Refer to the Sunflower block (page 82) to assemble the ring of pieces DD and EE. Sew the ring to the inner BB/CC circle, matching the points of pieces BB and EE. Refer to Hand Piecing Curves (page 57) as needed.

4. Refer to Octagon Compass, Step 5 (above) as needed to sew the Sunflower Star to piece AA. Match degree lines to points of DD.

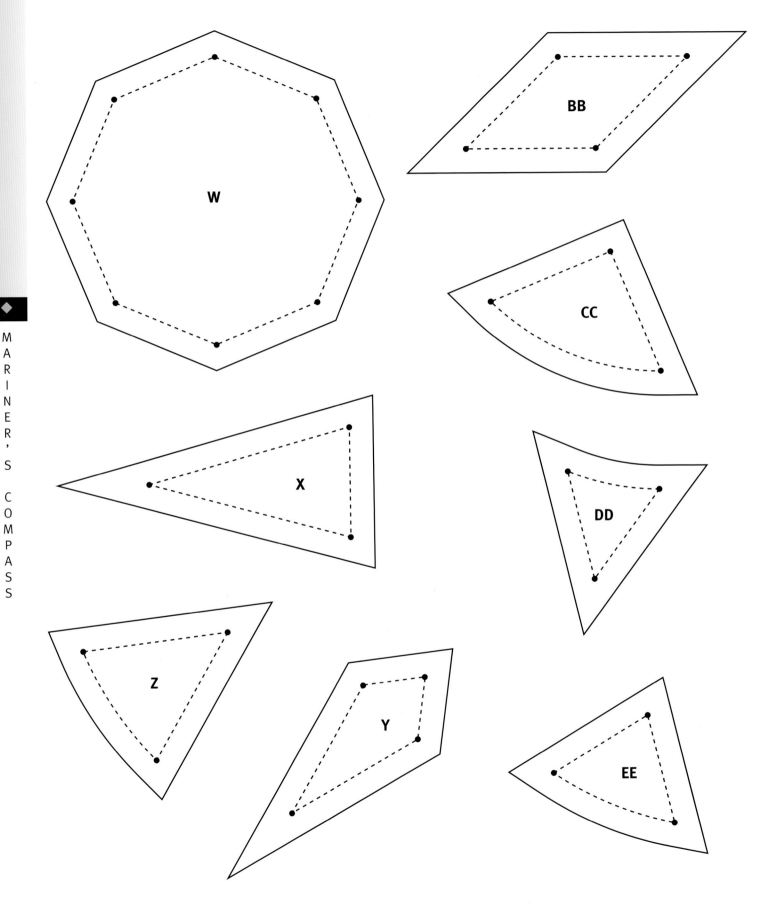

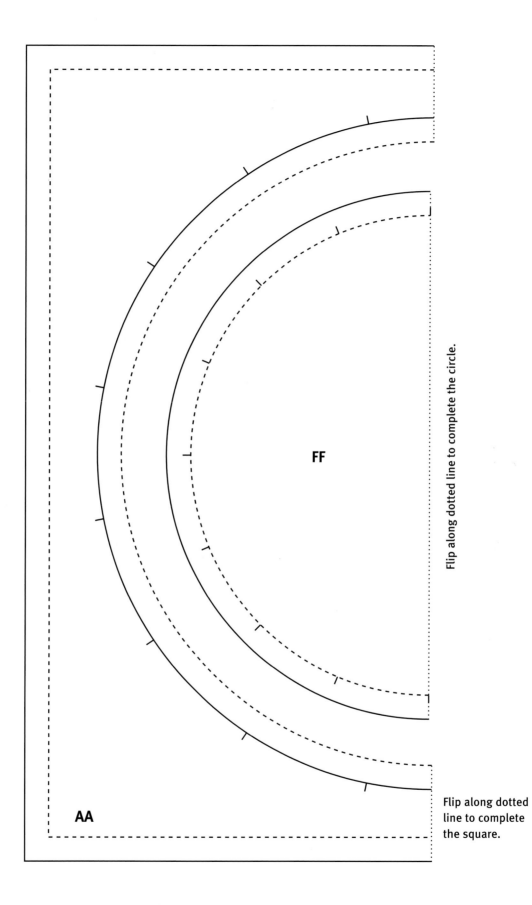

FF

AA

Flip along dotted line to complete the circle.

Flip along dotted line to complete the square.

Blue French

Pieced and quilted
by Inga-Lill Westblom

51" x 67"

Sunrise

Pieced and quilted
by Alice Watkins

64" x 74"

The Red Birds of Happiness

Pieced and hand quilted
by Karen Bacon

67" x 67"

SASHING OPTIONS

Sashing treatments unify and separate a sampling of quilt blocks.

ashing separates and enhances the blocks in a quilt. This chapter includes five sashing options. Before arranging your blocks, review Planning Your Quilt (page 8), and Fabric Selection (page 18). Also, study the quilts in this book, paying special attention to the sashing treatments.

Patterns appear on pages 92–93. You'll find layout guides in Planning Your Quilt (pages 12–14).

KEYS TO SUCCESS!

Lay the blocks in rows and label them before you assemble the sashing.

Option One

This option creates Evening Stars at the intersection of each block. The star points extend into the border area, which adds 1" to each side of the quilt.

Cutting

Cut pieces A, B, and C from your assorted fabrics. Cut pieces G, H, and N from the background fabric.

	A	B	C	G	H	N
9-Block Quilt	16	128	24	12	16	4
12-Block Quilt	20	160	31	14	18	4
25-Block Quilt	36	288	60	20	24	4

Assembly

1. Sew 4 piece B's to 1 piece C to create a rectangle. Sew a B/C unit to the top of every block. Sew B/C/block units into vertical rows. Sew an additional B/C unit to the *bottom block* of each row.

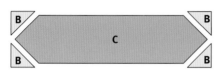

9-Block Quilt: Make 24
12-Block Quilt: Make 31
25-Block Quilt: Make 60

2. For the vertical sashing, sew B/C units to A (squares).

3. For the outer star points, sew 2 piece B's to 1 piece H.

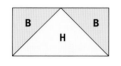

9-Block Quilt: Make 16
12-Block Quilt: Make 18
25-Block Quilt: Make 24

4. Sew H/B units and G pieces into vertical rows. Add 1 piece N to each end of the outside pieced sashing strips.

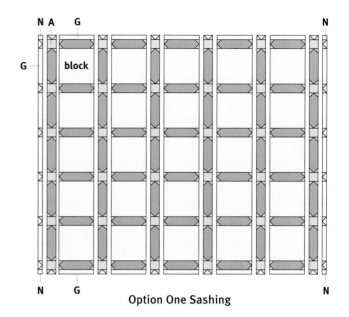

Option One Sashing

Option Two

This option is assembled in the same fashion as Option One, except the star points do not extend into the border area. As in Option One, cut pieces A, B, and C from your assorted fabrics.

Cutting

	A	B	C
9-Block Quilt	16	96	24
12-Block Quilt	20	124	31
25-Block Quilt	36	240	60

Option Three

Cutting

Piece E is cut from two different colors. Pieces H and I are cut from the background fabric.

	E	H	I
9-Block quilt	24 color a 24 color b	8	4
12-Block quilt	30 color a 32 color b	10	4
25-Block quilt	60 color a 60 color b	16	4

Assembly

1. Sew piece E, color a, to the top and bottom of alternate blocks in your layout. Sew piece E, color b, to the sides of these blocks.

2. Sew piece E, color b, to the top and bottom, and piece E, color a, to the sides. Alternate the blocks in your layout. Sew the blocks together into vertical rows, then sew the rows together.

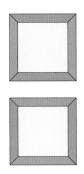

3. Sew alternately colored E and H pieces together, to achieve the required length. Colors will alternate with the blocks on the outside of the quilt to form E/H units. Sew these strips to the outside edges of the quilt.

4. Sew a piece I to each corner of the quilt.

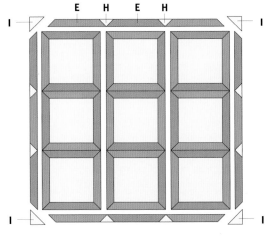

Option Three Sashing

Option Four

Instructions are for two alternating colors, similar to *A Graceful Waiting* (page 59).

Cutting

Piece F is cut from two different colors. H and I are cut from the background fabric.

	F	H	I
9-Block Quilt	12 color a 12 color b	8	4
12-Block Quilt	15 color a 16 color b	10	4
25-Block Quilt	30 color a 30 color b	16	4

Assembly

1. Sew piece F, color a, to the left and bottom sides of designated color a blocks in your arrangement. Sew piece F, color b, to the left and bottom sides of the designated color b blocks.

2. Sew piece H to the lower left side of each block, except the last block in the row on the left. Sew piece H to the lower right side of the last block in each row, except for the last row on the right.

3. Sew the blocks together into vertical rows and the sew the rows together.

4. Sew piece F's in the appropriate color order for the top and right sides of the quilt, adding piece H to form a strip. Sew the top and right side strips to the body of the quilt. Add piece I to each corner.

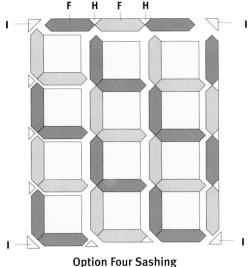

Option Four Sashing

Option Five

Cutting

	A	D
9-Block Quilt	16	24
12-Block Quilt	20	31
25-Block Quilt:	36	60

Assembly

1. Sew piece D to the top of each block. Sew a piece D to the bottom of the last block in each row. Sew the blocks together into vertical rows.

2. Sew pieces A and D together in vertical rows of the required length. Begin and end each row with piece A at each end. Sew the rows together.

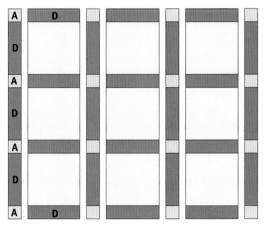

Option Five Sashing

Alternate Rotary Cutting Method

The number of pieces will vary with the number of blocks used. See the layout guides on pages 12–14.

Piece A: Cut 2 $\frac{1}{2}$"-wide strips. Cut the strips into 2 $\frac{1}{2}$" squares.

Unit B/C: Cut 1 rectangle 2 $\frac{1}{2}$" x 8 $\frac{1}{2}$" and 4 squares 1 $\frac{1}{2}$" x 1 $\frac{1}{2}$" for each sashing unit. Refer to Evening Star (page 66).

Piece D: Cut 2 $\frac{1}{2}$"-wide strips. Cut into 2 $\frac{1}{2}$" x 8 $\frac{1}{2}$" rectangles.

Piece E: Cut 1 $\frac{1}{2}$"-wide strips of two colors, then cut the strips into 1 $\frac{1}{2}$" x 11 $\frac{1}{4}$" rectangles, and then trim the short ends at a 45° angle in opposite directions to form a trapezoid. Refer to pattern on page 93 as needed.

Piece F: Cut 2 $\frac{1}{2}$"-wide strips. Cut the strips into 2 $\frac{1}{2}$" x 10 $\frac{3}{4}$" rectangles. Mark the two short ends with a dot at 1 $\frac{1}{2}$". Cut a 45° angle from the long sides to the dots to create a point. Refer to pattern on page 93 as needed.

Piece G: Cut 1 $\frac{1}{2}$"-wide strips. Cut the strips into 1 $\frac{1}{2}$" x 8 $\frac{1}{2}$" rectangles.

Piece H: Cut 1 square for every 4 triangles needed. Cut 3 $\frac{1}{4}$" squares. Cut each square twice diagonally.

Piece I: Cut 1 square for every 2 triangles needed. Cut 2 $\frac{7}{8}$" squares. Cut each square once diagonally.

Piece N: Cut 1 $\frac{1}{2}$"-wide strips. Cut into 1 $\frac{1}{2}$" squares.

SASHING TEMPLATE PATTERNS

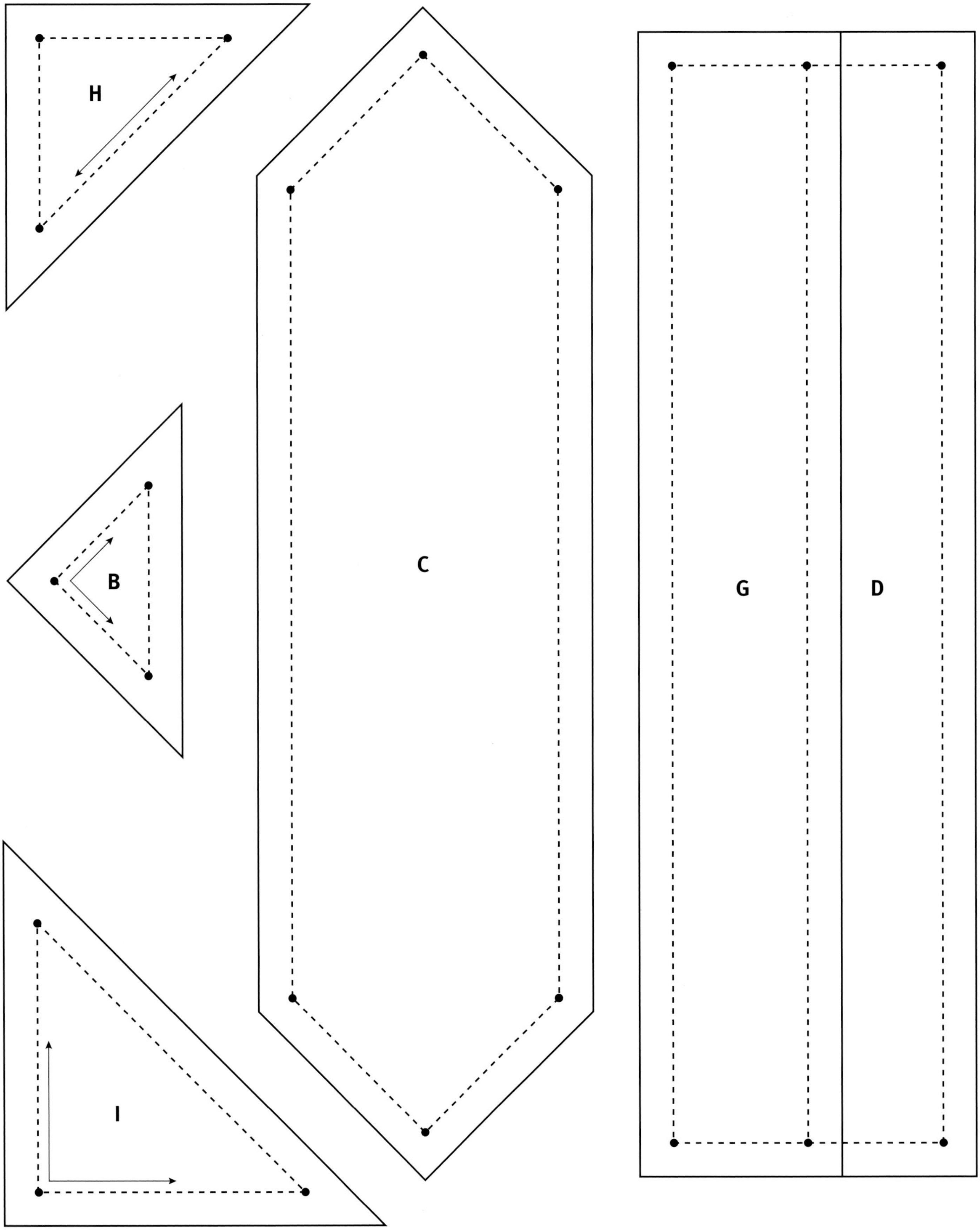

H

B

C

G

D

I

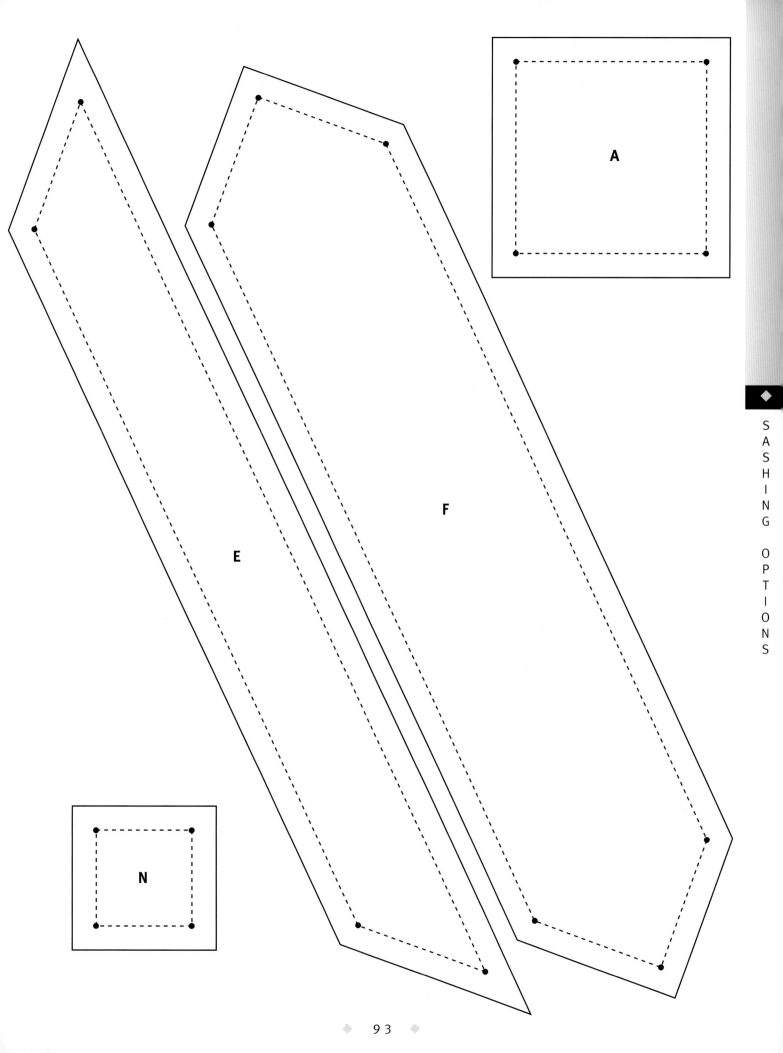

A

E

F

N

BORDERS

Frame a quilt with one of three appliqué border designs.

This chapter includes three appliqué borders with mitered corners: Swag and Teardrop, Vine and Leaf, and Dogtooth. All borders finish 8" wide. Before beginning, review Fabric Selection (page 18), and study the quilts throughout the book for inspiration. Yardage information appears on page 10.

Appliqué all the elements, except those that fall in the corners, prior to sewing the borders onto the quilt. Refer to the appliqué instructions and techniques in Appliqué (page 26).

Preparing the Border Strips

Use the same preparation methods for the border strips as you did for the blocks and sashing—either the marked seamline method or the rotary method. Working on a large work surface, measure the outside edges of your quilt.

Marked Seamline Method

1. On the wrong side of a single layer of 40"-wide fabric, mark 4 strips, 8 1/2" wide x the length required for your quilt *plus* 20". Use a yardstick and mechanical pencil to draw a line slightly longer than the length of the finished border along the selvage edge of the fabric. Mark the first seamline.

2. Use a gridded ruler to draw a line 8" from and parallel to the line you marked in the previous step. This is the second seamline. Lay a yardstick along this line and repeat to make four border strips. Rotary cut between the seamlines separating the borders.

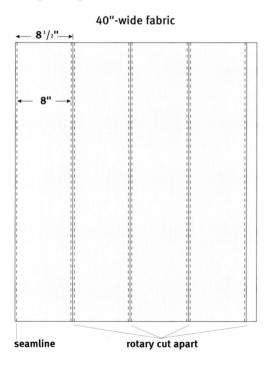

3. Use a Hera marker or a pencil to mark the finished length of the quilt top on each strip (point A).

4. Align a 12 1/2" square ruler with the marked seamline. Place the 8" line of the ruler at point A. Go up and over on the 8" ruler line, and place a mark at point B as shown. Draw a line from point A to point B. This is the miter's

seamline. *Do not* trim the seam allowance until the appliqué is completed and the borders have been added to the quilt body.

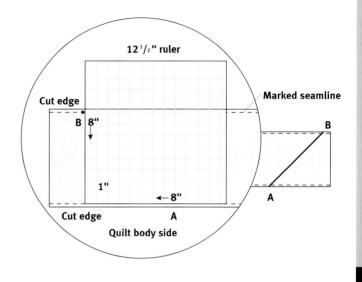

Cut Line Method

1. Cut borders from a 40"–wide fabric x the length of the quilt *plus* 20". Fold the selvage edges together and then fold again lengthwise to create 4 layers. Working on a large surface, smooth and crease the folds. Align a 6" x 24" cutting ruler to the folds and cut along the selvage edge.

2. Align a 12 1/2" square ruler along the cut (selvage) edge and cut 8 1/2" from that edge. *Do not* cut miters until the appliqué is completed and the borders have been added to the quilt body.

Swag and Teardrop Border

Make plastic templates of the side, corner, and teardrop patterns on page 99. Mark and cut the necessary fabric pieces. Fussy cut large prints for a stunning effect. Prepare the border background as described above.

1. Along the sides of the border strips that attach to the quilt body, mark the placement of the swags with a crease or pin. Mark 1" from each end and 1/2" in from the seamline. Divide and mark the remaining space into 10" increments.

2. Place the swag fabric right side up on a sandpaper board to stabilize it. Place the swag template on the fabric and trace around it with a white or silver pencil.

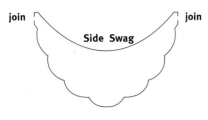

3. Cut out the swag pieces, adding a $^1/_8$"-wide seam allowance, except at the swag join. The side swags measure exactly 10" wide and align at the center of each sashing intersection.

4. Transfer the seamlines to the right side of the border by placing pins at regular intervals. Leave a $^3/_4$" margin from the finished tips of the swags to the pin-marked seamline. Pin, baste, and appliqué the swags to the borders.

5. Pin, baste, and appliqué the teardrops to cover the swag joins. Place the rounded end of the teardrop $^1/_2$" from the seamline of the outer edge of the border that joins the border to the body of the quilt.

6. Sew the borders to the sides of the quilt. Miter the corners and trim the seam allowances to $^1/_4$".

7. Pin, baste, and appliqué the corner swags, aligning the raw edges of the side and the corner swags. Appliqué the teardrops to cover the raw edges where the swags join.

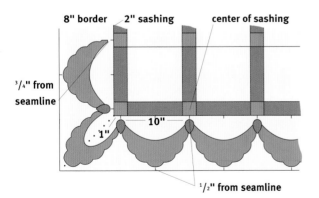

Dogtooth Border

Refer to the layout on page 13. Prepare the border backgrounds following the instructions on page 95.

1. From the lengthwise grain of the fabric, rotary cut 4 strips 2 $^1/_2$" by the length of the borders, plus 4". These strips become the dogtooth appliqué, *and include the $^1/_4$"-wide seam allowance.* Save the remaining fabric for the straight binding.

2. Align a dogtooth strip to the outside edge of the border background as shown below, leaving an extra 2" at each end. Baste together along the outside edge only.

3. Mark each end of each dogtooth strip by placing a silk pin on the longest (outside edge) seamline (point A), from the backside of the border background through to the dogtooth strip.

4. Align the 2 $^1/_2$" line of a square ruler with point A and the cut edge of the dogtooth strip. Go up and over on the 2 $^1/_2$" line, and mark a dot, $^1/_4$" down from the cut edge of the dogtooth strip (point B).

5. From the first dot, use a small ruler to measure and mark dots at $^3/_4$" increments $^1/_4$" down from the cut edge. Work toward the center of the dogtooth strip 6" at a time.

6. Leave approximately 14" unmarked at the center of the dogtooth strip. Measure to estimate if the remaining dots will fit this area evenly. If not, adjust the spacing very slightly. Finish marking the dots.

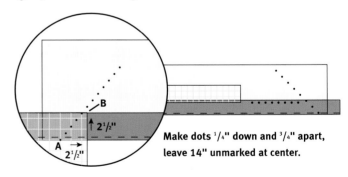

Make dots $^1/_4$" down and $^3/_4$" apart, leave 14" unmarked at center.

7. Align a small ruler to the first dot. Draw a 1" line at a 90° angle to the cut edge at each end of the dogtooth strip. Skip the second dot. Mark the third dot, skip the fourth dot, and so on. Work from both ends of the strip in 6" increments.

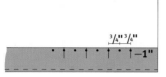

8. It's best to work one dogtooth at a time. Cut on the drawn lines, keeping the cuts perpendicular and even. Fold and crease from the base of the first cut to the first dot (Step A). Fold under the ¼" seam allowance at the point (Step B), then fold and crease from the point to the base of the second cut to complete the point (Step C). Pin to hold.

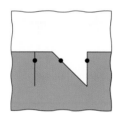

Step A: Fold dot to dot.

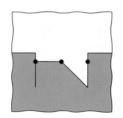

Step B: Fold under ¼".

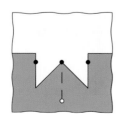

Step C: Fold dot to dot.

9. Begin appliquéing midway along the side of the first fold. Appliqué up to the point, half way down the next side, and then stop. Fold, pin, and appliqué one dogtooth at a time. Refer to Inside Points and Outside Points, pages 33-34, as needed. After all four borders are appliquéd, join them to the quilt.

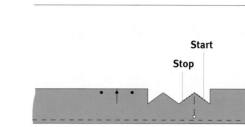

10. To transfer the mitered seamline from the back of the border background to the top of the dogtooth strip, align the strip with the cut edge of the border background and pin. Place right side down on a cutting mat. Using the seamlines as a guide, lay a ruler on the line and use a Hera marker to make a crease. Repeat for each strip.

11. Pin the creased dogtooth strips out of the way while you stitch the border's mitered corner seam. Trim the seam allowance to ¼" and press. Repeat for each corner.

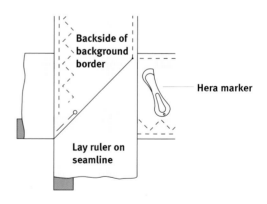

12. Pin the creased seamlines of the dogtooth strips together and stitch. Trim the excess fabric to a ¼"-wide seam allowance. Repeat for each corner. Fold under the unstitched corners of the dogtooth strips and crease. Appliqué the corner to the background border.

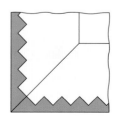

Vine and Leaf Border

Use the pattern on page 99. Refer to the layout on page 12. Prepare the border backgrounds following the instructions on page 95. Use assorted fabrics for the leaves.

1. Follow the directions for marking the Swag and Teardrop border (page 95). In addition, make creased markings, or place pins, on the outside edges of the borders, spacing them evenly between the 10" marks.

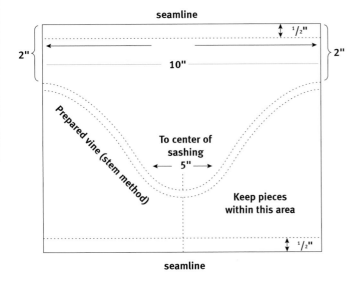

2. Cut bias strips 1 1/4" wide and as long as possible. Refer to Preparing Stems (page 29) to prepare a long vine. Join the vines together in lengths that equal the outside of each border plus an additional 30".

3. Use a pin to mark 4" from the end of each border, and 2" from the seamline. Position and baste the vines using these marked guides.

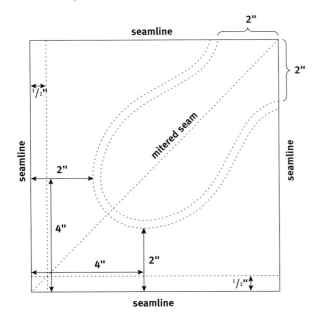

4. Make a plastic template for the leaf. Mark, cut, and prepare 16 leaves for each block along the borders and 16 for each corner. Space leaves evenly at the same angle for each outer and inner curve and at the four corners.

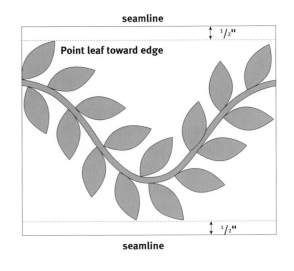

5. Appliqué the vines and leaves to the border strips, leaving the corner leaves and vines unstitched for now. Sew the borders to the quilt, stitching the mitered corner seams. Trim the seam allowance to 1/4" and press. Appliqué the vines and leaves in each corner. To join the ends of the vines, unfold each end, seam them together at a 45° angle, refold, and finish appliquéing.

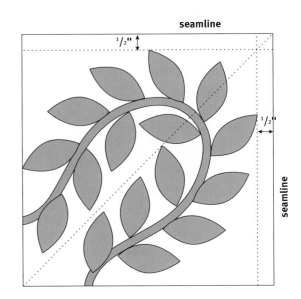

BORDER PATTERNS

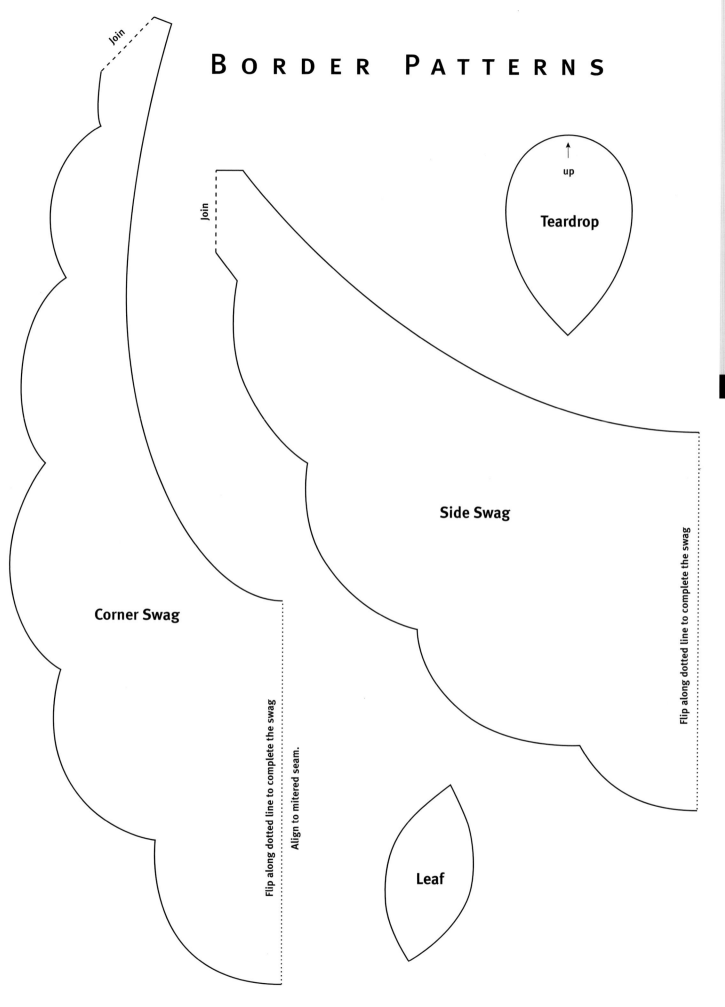

Join

Teardrop

up

Join

Side Swag

Corner Swag

Flip along dotted line to complete the swag

Flip along dotted line to complete the swag

Align to mitered seam.

Leaf

Blue Birds of Paradise
Pieced and quilted
by Nellie Bomer
48" x 62"

Spring Fling
Pieced and quilted
by Juanita Benoit
54" x 54"

HAND QUILTING

Quilting stitches add visual interest and beautiful texture to quilts.

Quilting stitches define your appliqué and patchwork with secondary design, create visual interest in the background areas, and add overall texture to your quilt. Choose a quilting pattern that enhances your appliqué and patchwork, rather than compete with them. I enjoy the process of hand quilting, as well as the beautiful textural results. This chapter includes information to refine your skills and to enhance the experience.

KEYS TO SUCCESS!

Prewash fabrics to soften them for hand-stitching.
Use 100% cotton quilting thread with cotton fabrics.
Use fresh, fine needles for even stitches.
Good lighting is essential!

Preparing the Top & Backing

Add a 6"-wide strip of waste fabric to all four sides of the quilt top. (I use bargain fabrics or muslin.) Stitch on the seamline using a normal stitch length. The added strips extend the amount of fabric held in the quilt hoop or frame, making it easier to stitch to the edges of the quilt. After you finish quilting, remove the waste fabric strips and reuse them on the next quilt.

If you washed the fabrics for the quilt top, then prewash and press the backing fabric as well. Depending on the width of your quilt, you may need to seam two or more lengths of fabric, or purchase wider fabric made especially for backings. Always use 100% cotton fabrics suitable for quiltmaking—not sheets or decorator fabrics which can be difficult to needle. I select fabrics with dramatic or large-scale prints that complement the style of the quilt top.

When you prepare the backing, be sure to add a minimum of 6" on each side.

Selecting and Preparing Batting

Buy the best quality batting that you can afford. Read the package instructions carefully, as it typically includes information about prewashing, and suggests quilting density. As a rule, it is easier to hand quilt prewashed cotton batting. Some quiltmakers prefer a tightly-drawn look to their quilts, so instead of prewashing the batting, they wash the finished quilt. At least two days prior to basting your quilt, unfold the batting and allow it to "relax."

Hobbs batting is my favorite. I use their 100% wool batting for hand quilting intricate designs, and I do not prewash it. When I plan less detailed quilting, I prefer 100% bleached cotton which I prewash. Whichever batting you choose, cut it several inches larger than the quilt top all around, so it extends into the waste fabric.

Layering and Basting

I prefer to thread baste my quilts. No matter which basting method you choose, press both the quilt top and backing before you begin.

KEYS TO SUCCESS!

Basting with a group of friends makes the process more fun. Plan a day to work on one or more quilts together. Invite enough people to bring the ingredients for a good taco salad and meet at a facility that has several large, scratch-resistant tables that you can push together to make a large surface. A "Basting Party" offers a fine reason to gather, stitch, and enjoy good food. Just be sure to keep the food far from the quilts!

Use masking tape to affix the backing fabric wrong side up on a clean table. Layer and gently smooth the batting on top of the backing, working from the center toward the outer edges. Center the quilt top, right side up on the batting. Again, gently smooth the layers, working from the center to the outer edges.

Always begin and end basting in the waste fabric. Use a long darner needle and a spoon, and begin basting along one side of the quilt. Baste in a grid pattern, taking large 2"-long stitches. I follow the straight of grain or the lines of the quilt blocks as a guide and baste 3"–3 1/2" apart in both directions.

When the quilt is completely grid-basted, bring the edge of the backing around to the front of the quilt top, fold over, and baste in place. This covers the edges of the batting and protects them while you quilt.

KEYS TO SUCCESS!

Basting is easy when you use a long darner needle and a spoon. Place the spoon in front of the tip of the needle. As the needle emerges from the under side of the quilt, the tip of the needle easily slides into the bowl of the spoon.

Quilting Design Basics

I recommend traditional quilting designs for these traditional Perfect Union quilts. Focus on designs that unify the straightline patchwork and flowing appliqués. Study the quilts in the book for numerous examples.

Avoid quilting through seam allowances.

Cable or feather designs traced from pre-made quilting stencils are especially effective for quilting Dogtooth borders and sashing areas. See Resources (page 110) for information on where to purchase stencils.

Quilting lines can unify appliqué and patchwork.

Begin quilting directly along the outside edges of the appliqués ("in the ditch"). Unless they are large, do not quilt inside the appliqué pieces. Echo quilting, straight lines, diagonal lines, or cross-hatching work well for the background surrounding appliqué. These lines add texture and make the background fabric recede while pushing the appliqué forward.

Quilting stencils are ideal for borders and sashings.

Quilting the background makes it recede.

There are many ways to quilt a patchwork block. The most important thing to remember is to avoid stitching through seam allowances wherever possible.

Marking Your Quilt

I mark a quilt *after* it is basted. Test your marking tool on fabric scraps from the quilt prior to actually marking the quilt top. Mark all straight lines or grids using Scotch Magic tape and an acrylic ruler, or use a Hera marker.

When I use a stencil, I use a Hera marker or light pencil *just before* quilting the area. For the best results, tape the stencil in place with masking tape, and then mark *lightly*. Good stitching covers the pencil lines, eliminating the need to remove them. If needed, use a white eraser to remove the lines immediately after the stitching is completed.

You may also use the fabric's print as a stitching guide. In many of my patchwork blocks and border swags, I outline-quilt large flowers or paisley designs.

Outline-quilt following the fabric's design.

Quilting Tools and Supplies

There are many wonderful quilting tools available, and every quiltmaker discovers those she likes the best. I have included those that I consider essential for hand quilting. See Resources (page 110) for additional information.

Hoop

A 14" wooden quilting hoop is an ideal size for most quilters. Determine the size best for you by placing the hoop on your arm, close to the elbow. If the hoop reaches to your palm, it will probably be a comfortable size for you. Another choice is to use an 11" x 17" plastic tube frame.

Thimble

You may need to try a few to find the one you like the best. With time, any thimble becomes comfortable, as long as it fits. I use one with a raised ridge to grip the eye of the needle for the rocking stitch. Choose a thimble that will not fall off your finger easily. I have discovered a "thimble" made by the House of Quilting that "you hold instead of wear."

Thread

My favorite is 100% cotton quilting thread made by YLI. It is strong and finished with a glorious glaze that does not tangle and slips easily through fabrics and battings. Quilting threads with rough surfaces can cause batting fiber to migrate, or "beard," to the surface.

Whether the design is intricate or consists of straight grid lines, quilting creates a shadow. A very light color quilting thread erases—or certainly minimizes—the shadow. Use quilting thread at least two shades darker than the background fabric. For quilts with a range of values, from very dark to fairly light, use thread in a medium, neutral color. If the quilt is primarily cool-colored, use a medium gray. If the quilt is mostly warm in color, use a medium brown or tan. A medium-value thread appears lighter than it does on the spool. You may wish to avoid high contrast: A nearly white thread stitched across a very dark fabric may not complement your quilt.

Needles

A Between needle is most commonly used for hand quilting. Brands vary in thickness and length. The higher the number, the shorter the needle: #12 is the shortest. I recommend that you work with an #11 or smaller needle. My favorite needle is an EZ brand Gold-Eye Between in size #12. The gold-eye feature makes it easier to thread.

Quilting (Stitching Basics)

Always quilt from the center of your quilt to the outer edges. Place your basted quilt in the hoop with the back as taut as the top, but not tight as a drum. If needed, loosen all three layers just a little by using your hand to put a little pressure in the center of the hoop. The slightly loosened tension makes it easier to manipulate the needle. When you are satisfied, tighten the wing nut on the hoop.

Thread the needle with an 18"-long, single strand of thread. Knot one end, leaving a 1 1/2" tail. Insert the needle through the quilt top and batting (not into the backing) about 1" from where you want to start stitching. Gently pull the thread until the knot pops through the fabric and into the batting.

Hold the hoop in a comfortable position and stitch toward yourself, turning the hoop as needed. Hold the needle between your thumb and index finger (your "needle hand"). Put the needle straight down into the quilt at the point where you want to begin stitching. Place your other hand (your "underneath hand") under the quilt so that you can feel the needle tip with each stitch. This is where a callus helps!

Rock the needle up and down to take small, even stitches through all three layers of the quilt. Place 3 to 5 stitches on your needle at once.

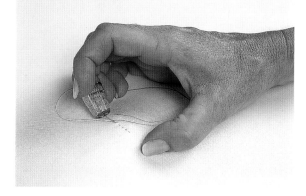

Right-handed

End a row of quilting from the top side of your quilt. Wrap the thread around the tip of the needle once to create a slipknot. Draw the knot to the end of the thread, near the top of the quilt. Insert the needle between the layers and gently pull the thread to pop the knot inside the batting. Carefully trim the thread and gently lift or rub the quilt top fabric. This allows the thread tail to disappear into the quilt.

Remove all basting stitches, and trim the outside edges of the quilt. Use the final seamline to align a cutting ruler and allow for 1/4"-wide seam allowances.

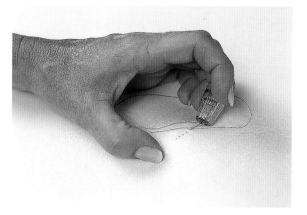

Left-handed

Albert's Mourning Stars
Pieced and quilted
by Joan Northern
44" x 44"

My Blue Heaven
Pieced by Eloise Vannoy,
hand quilted
by Kara Kasberg
55" x 67"

FINISHING

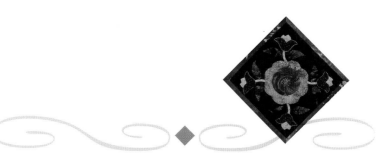

A quilt is not complete until it is labeled and bound.

Labels

Quilt labels include welcome documentation for those who view your quilts in the future. I like making photo transfer labels that resemble glorious picture frames. I use Dover Publications, Inc. books, available in print and CD-ROM format, as a resource. My favorite titles include *Old Fashioned Frames*, *Art Nouveau Frames*, and *Decorative Wreaths and Frames* (see Resources, page 110). These books include hundreds of designs to trace by hand or print onto fabric with a computer.

Quilt label resembles a picture frame.

Preparing Labels by Hand

Photocopy and enlarge the frame of your choice. Press a piece of freezer paper, shiny side down, to the back of the label fabric to stabilize it. Use a light box to trace the pattern onto your fabric with a permanent marker. Add your message inside the frame.

Preparing Labels Using a Computer

Use a software program that allows you to insert clip art from a disk and insert a text box inside the clip art area. I use The Print Shop 10.

Follow the product instructions to prepare the label fabric with a product such as Bubble Jet Set®. Press the prepared fabric to a sheet of freezer paper to stabilize it, and trim to $8 \frac{1}{2}$" x 11". You can print more than one label on a single fabric sheet.

KEYS TO SUCCESS!

Transfer a photo of yourself onto a disk at a photo shop or via a digital camera. Use your computer to transfer the photo to your label.

Trace around the inside opening of a precut rectangular or oval framing mat to mark seamlines. Trim to $\frac{1}{8}$"-wide seam allowance, add your message, and apply your label.

Binding

1. I use $\frac{3}{8}$"-wide finished, double-fold binding to finish my quilts. To make this binding, cut $2 \frac{1}{4}$"-wide bias or straight-grain fabric strips. Cut enough strips to go around the perimeter of the quilt, plus 14" for mitering corners. Sew the strips together into one continuous strip using diagonal seams. Fold the strip in half lengthwise, wrong sides together, and press. Turn under one end of the strip at a 45° angle and press.

2. Starting at the center of one side of the quilt, place the binding on the front of the quilt, aligning the raw edges of the binding and the raw edges of the quilt. Pin in place. Sew the binding to the quilt with a $\frac{1}{4}$"-wide seam allowance, leaving the first few inches of binding loose so you can join the beginning and ending of the binding

strip later. Be careful not to stretch the quilt or the binding as you sew. When you reach a corner, stop stitching $\frac{1}{4}$" from the edge and backstitch. Trim the thread.

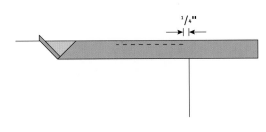

Stitch to $\frac{1}{4}$" from corner.

3. Rotate the quilt so you can stitch the next side. Fold the binding up and away from the quilt and then fold it back onto itself, parallel with the edge of the quilt. Start stitching at the corner with a backstitch to create an angled fold at the corner.

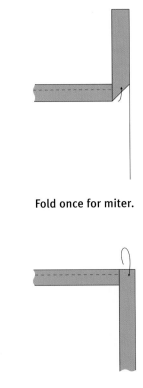

Fold once for miter.

Fold again for alignment. Start stitching at folded edge.

4. Continue stitching around the quilt, repeating the process at each corner. When you reach the starting point, overlap the ends about 1", and trim the excess binding at a 45° angle. Tuck the raw end into the fold and finish the seam.

5. Fold the binding to the back of the quilt, covering the seam, and blind stitch in place. Blind stitch the mitered corners—quilt judges like this!

KEYS TO SUCCESS!

For single-fold bias binding, I use the Clover Tape Maker which comes with excellent instructions for its use. It makes perfect creases for aligning the binding to the front and the back of the quilt. and is available to create binding in a variety of widths (see Resources on page 110).

Piped Cording Combined with Binding

I added a narrow piped cording (cotton, size 50) just inside the binding of *A Perfect Union* (page 7).

1. Cut 1 ¹/₄"-wide strips of fabric on the straight grain or bias. Using diagonal seams, sew the strips together to create four lengths, each matching the measurement of a side of the quilt. Cover the narrow cording with the strip of fabric (right sides out) and baste close to the cording by hand or with the zipper or cording foot on your machine.

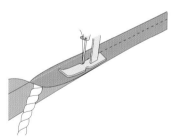

2. At the corners, fold back the piping fabric, and trim the cording so it does not extend into the seam allowance. Trim the piping fabric even with the quilt edge. Trim the cording at the beginning end of the piping, and butt the cord to the previous piping strip, overlapping the seam allowances only. The seam allowance for each covered cord should extend to the cut edge of the quilt.

Trim cording ¹/₄"

3. Use a zipper foot to attach the binding next to the piping. Follow the instructions for bindings to complete.

Hanging Your Quilt

1. Cut a fabric strip 8" x the width of the quilt *plus* 1"–2". Hem the ends so that the finished width of the sleeve is slightly shorter than the width of the quilt. Fold the fabric strip in half lengthwise, wrong sides together. Sew the long raw edges together with a ¹/₄"-wide seam. Fold the tube so the seam is centered on one side.

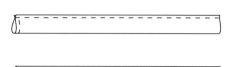

2. Pin the sleeve seam side down on the back side of the quilt, 1" from the top-edge binding. Hand sew the top and bottom edges of the sleeve to the quilt. Avoid catching the front of the quilt as you stitch.

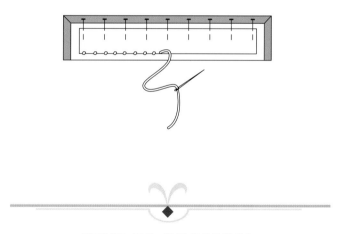

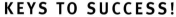

KEYS TO SUCCESS!

Before stitching the bottom edge of the sleeve, push the sleeve up so the sleeve covers about half of the binding. Pin and stitch the bottom edge of the sleeve. This provides a little "give" so the hanging rod does not put a strain on the quilt.

RESOURCES

Nancy's Quilt Block
1412 N. Valley Mills
Waco, TX 76710
Phone: (254) 776-4989
E-mail: NANQUBLOCK@prodigy.net

The Sewing Basket
525 N. Stagecoach Drive
Salado, TX 76571
Phone: (877) 244-0450
E-mail: sewbskt@vvm.com
Website: www.thesewingbasket.com

Cotton Patch Mail Order
1025 Hall Lane, Dept. CTB
Lafayette, CA 94549
Phone: (800) 835-4418 or (925) 283-7883
E-mail: quiltusa@yahoo.com
Website: www.quiltusa.com

Hand-Dyed and Ethnic Fabrics
Leo9 Textiles
PO Box 150033
Austin, TX 78722
Phone: (512) 472-1655
E-mail: Leo9@texas.net

For information about Hobbs Batting:
Hobbs Bonded Fibers
200 S Commerce Drive
Waco, TX 76710
Customer Service: (800) 433-3357
E-mail: hdwilbanks@hobbsbondedfibers.com
Website: http://hobbsbondedfibers.com/

Sample Sets of Hobbs Batting
Hancock's of Paducah
3841 Hinkleville Road
Paducah, KY 42001
Phone: (800) 845-8723
Website and catalog requests:
www.Hancocks-Paducah.com

Metal Templates
Quiltsmith
252 Cedar Road
Poquoson, VA 23662-2112
Phone: (800) 982-7326
E-mail: sales@ardcotemplates.com
Website: www.ardcotemplates.com

For book, fabric, and seminar information:
Jinny Beyer
776 Walker Road, Suite E
Great Falls, VA 22066
Phone: (703) 759-0250
E-mail: info@jinnybeyer.com
Website: www.jinnybeyer.com

For book, and plastic template information:
Marti Michell
3525 Broad Street
Chamblee, GA 30341
Phone: (770) 458-6500
E-mail: cs@frommarti.com (customer service)
Website: www.frommarti.com

For quilting stencils:
Stencil Company
28 Castlewood Drive
Cheektowaga, NY 14227
Phone: (716) 656-9430
E-mail: info@quiltingstencils.com
Website: www.quiltingstencils.com

For "The Thimble That You Hold
Instead of Wear":
House of Quilting
Route 31, Box 5721
Fayetteville, NC 28306
Phone: (910) 868-3842

For clip art books and CD-ROMs:
Dover Publications, Inc.
31 East 2nd Street
Mineola, NY 11501
Website: www.doverpublications.com
Ask for their Clip Art Catalog (58363-5)

For Mariner's Compass books and
workshop information:
Judy Mathieson
1977 Green Hill Road
Sebastopol, CA 95472
Phone: (707) 823-4522
E-mail: judy4quilt@aol.com
Website: members.aol.com/judy4quilt

For printing quilt label information:
Bubble Jet Set ®
C. Jenkins Necktie Company
St. Louis, MO 63135
Phone: (314) 521-7544

My wonderful machine quilters:
Julie Zentell
1405 Hummingbird Drive
Hillsboro, TX 76645
Phone: (254) 582-0654
E-mail: zentell2@netscape.net

Sue Miklos-Champion
403 E. Preston Glen Road
Gunter, TX 75058
Phone: (903) 433-9303
E-mail: champion_miklos@msn.com

My wonderful quilt photographer:
Bob Smith
Accurate Image of Waco Texas
2919 Mary
Waco, TX 76710
Phone: (254) 756-3977
E-mail: bob@accurateimage.org
Website:
http://www.accurateimage.org

ABOUT THE AUTHOR

Darlene C. Christopherson started quiltmaking in 1979 as a stay-at-home mother, living in Sterling, Virginia. She began teaching quilting classes in 1982 and for five years, was also on the staff of the Jinny Beyer Hilton Head Island Seminar. In 1992, after she and her family (husband Doug and daughter Pilar) moved to their hometown of Sioux Falls, South Dakota, Darlene began teaching at the national level. She and her family moved to China Spring (Waco), Texas in 1997 and Darlene continues to teach hand appliqué and quilting classes across the country.

Darlene creates and publishes patterns for small hand appliqué projects as well as for baby quilts. Her *Bankys*, kits for baby quilts, are a departure from her normal appliqué designs.

Several of Darlene's quilts have been published in quilting books, including *Sensational Scrap Quilts*, by Darra Duffy Williamson; *Soft-Edged Piecing*, and *Patchwork Portfolio*, by Jinny Beyer; *Scrap Quilts Fast and Fun*, and *Great American Quilts 1998* published by Oxmoor House; and *More Vertical Quilts with Style*, by Bobbie Aug and Sharon Newman.

Her quilts have been featured in *Quilting Today* (Issues 90, 96, and 98); *Traditional Quiltworks* (Issue 35); *Quilter's Newsletter Magazine* (May 2000 and November 1996); *Traditional Quilter* (July 1997).

Darlene has hosted appliqué retreats with Patricia B. Campbell. An article in the first issue of *Appliqué Quilts* shares that experience and some of their works. Darlene is a member of the American Quilter's Society, The National Quilting Association, The Appliqué Society, The Baltimore Appliqué Society, and her local guild in Waco, Texas.

INDEX

Appliqué 26
 Cutwork 27
 Pictorial 29
 Needle-Turn Stitch 32
Batting 102
Binding 108
Borders 94
 Swag and Teardrop 95
 Dogtooth 97
 Vine and Leaf 98
Eight-Pointed Star Variations 74
Embroidery Stitches 34
Evening Star Variations 60
Fabric Selection 18
Fussy Cutting 55
Hand Quilting 101
Hanging Sleeve 109
Labels 107
Mariner's Compass Variations 81

Needle-Turn Stitch 32
Patchwork 54
Piped Cording 109
Pressing 34
Quilt Finishing 107
Quilt Layouts 12
Quilt Planning 8
Quilting Tools and Supplies 104
Quilts
 Adventure into Appliqué and Patchwork, An 24
 Albert's Mourning Stars 106
 Anna's Influence 5
 Blue Birds of Paradise 100
 Blue French 86
 Dawn's Influence 73
 Empty Nest 4
 Encompassing Sunflowers 80
 Few of My Favorite Things, A 53

First Spring of the New Millennium, The 51
Graceful Waiting, A 59
Midnight Madness 52
My Blue Heaven 106
My Perfect Union 79
Never Say Never 58
Perfect Union, A 7
Perfect Union – Jennifer and Taylor, A 16
Perfect Union – My Salvation, The 17
Perfect Union Too, A 25
Perfectly Challenging 15
Red Birds of Happiness, The 87
Red is Cool 58
Searching for Solace 23
Spring Fling 100
Stars and Its Many Wonders 15

Sunrise 87
Whimsical Christmas, A 79
Sashing Options 88
Tools and Supplies 11, 104

OTHER FINE BOOKS
FROM C&T PUBLISHING

15 Two-Block Quilts: Unlock the Secrets of Secondary Patterns, Claudia Olson

Add on Seam Allowance Chart for Rotary Cutting and Drafting Templates©, Nancy Johnson-Srebro

All About Quilting from A to Z, from the Editors and Contributors of *Quilter's Newsletter Magazine* and *Quiltmaker Magazine*

Appliqué 12 Easy Ways!: Charming Quilts, Giftable Projects, & Timeless Techniques, Elly Sienkiewicz

Appliqué Inside the Lines: 12 Quilt Projects to Embroider & Appliqué, Carol Armstrong

Art of Classic Quiltmaking, The, Harriet Hargrave & Sharyn Craig

Art of Machine Piecing, The: How to Achieve Quality Workmanship Through a Colorful Journey, Sally Collins

Baltimore Beauties and Beyond Vol. l: Studies In Classic Album Quilt Appliqué, Elly Sienkiewicz

Beautifully Quilted with Alex Anderson: • How to Choose or Create the Best Designs for Your Quilt • 6 Timeless Projects • Full-Size Patterns, Ready to Use, Alex Anderson

Best of Baltimore Beauties, The: 95 Patterns for Album Blocks and Borders, Elly Sienkiewicz

Best of Baltimore Beauties Part II, The: More Patterns for Album Blocks, Elly Sienkiewicz

Block Magic, Too!: Over 50 NEW Blocks from Squares and Rectangles, Nancy Johnson-Srebro

Contemporary Classics in Plaids & Stripes: 9 Projects from Piece 'O Cake Designs, Linda Jenkins & Becky Goldsmith

Curves in Motion: Quilt Designs & Techniques, Judy Dales

Dresden Flower Garden: A New Twist on Two Quilt Classics, Blanche Young

Endless Possibilities: Using No-Fail Methods, Nancy Johnson-Srebro

Fancy Appliqué: 12 Lessons to Enhance Your Skills, Elly Sienkiewicz

From Fiber to Fabric: The Essential Guide to Quiltmaking Textiles, Harriet Hargrave

Hand Appliqué with Alex Anderson: Seven Projects for Hand Appliqué, Alex Anderson

Hand Quilting with Alex Anderson: Six Projects for First-Time Hand Quilters, Alex Anderson

Jacobean Rhapsodies: Composing with 28 Appliqué Designs, Pat Campbell & Mimi Ayers

Kaleidoscopes & Quilts, Paula Nadelstern

Lone Star Quilts and Beyond: Step-by-Step Projects and Inspiration, Jan Krentz

Luscious Landscapes: Simple Techniques for Dynamic Quilts, Joyce Becker

Mary Mashuta's Confetti Quilts: A No-Fuss Approach to Color, Fabric & Design, Mary Mashuta

Mastering Machine Appliqué, 2nd Edition: The Complete Guide Including: • Invisible Machine Appliqué • Satin Stitch • Blanket Stitch & Much More, Harriet Hargrave

Mastering Quilt Marking: Marking Tools and Techniques, Choosing Stencils, Matching Borders and Corners, Pepper Cory

Measure the Possibilities with Omnigrid®, Nancy Johnson-Srebro

New Sampler Quilt, The, Diana Leone

New England Museum Quilts, The, Jennifer Gilbert

Paper Piecing Potpourri: Fun-Filled Projects for Every Quilter, from the Editors and Contributors of *Quilter's Newsletter Magazine & Quiltmaker Magazine*

Patchwork Quilts Made Easy - Revised, 2nd Edition: 33 Quilt Favorites, Old & New, Jean Wells

Photo Transfer Handbook, The: Snap It, Print It, Stitch It!, Jean Ray Laury

Q is for Quilt, Diana McClun & Laura Nownes

Quilts, Quilts, and More Quilts!, Diana McClun & Laura Nownes

Radiant New York Beauties: 14 Paper-Pieced Quilt Projects, Valori Wells

Reverse Appliqué with No Brakez, Jan Mullen

Rotary Cutting with Alex Anderson: Tips, Techniques, and Projects, Alex Anderson

Setting Solutions, Sharyn Craig

Shoreline Quilts: Glorious Get-Away Projects, compiled by Cyndy Rymer

Simple Fabric Folding for Christmas: 14 Festive Quilts & Projects, Liz Aneloski

Slice of Christmas from Piece O' Cake Designs, A, Linda Jenkins & Becky Goldsmith

Soft-Edge Piecing: Add the Elegance of Appliqué to Traditional-Style Patchwork Design, Jinny Beyer

Wine Country Quilts: A Bounty of Flavorful Projects for Any Palette, Cyndy Rymer & Jennifer Rounds

For more information, write for a free catalog:
C&T Publishing, Inc.
P.O. Box 1456
Lafayette, CA 94549
(800) 284-1114
E-mail: ctinfo@ctpub.com
Website: www.ctpub.com

For quilting supplies:
Cotton Patch Mail Order
3405 Hall Lane, Dept.CTB
Lafayette, CA 94549
(800) 835-4418
(925) 283-7883
E-mail:quiltusa@yahoo.com
Website: www.quiltusa.com

Note: Fabrics used in the quilts shown may not be currently available since fabric manufacturers keep most fabrics in print for only a short time.